the Unofficial Guide® to Walt Disney World for Grown-Ups

1st Edition

Also available from Macmillan Travel:

Beyond Disney: The Unofficial Guide to Universal Studios, Sea World, and the Best of Central Florida, by Amber Morris and Bob Sehlinger

Inside Disney: The Incredible Story of Walt Disney World and the Man Behind the Mouse, by Eve Zibart

Mini-Mickey: The Pocket-Sized Unofficial Guide to Walt Disney World, by Bob Sehlinger

The Unofficial Guide to Bed & Breakfasts in New England, by Lea Lane

The Unofficial Guide to Branson, Missouri, by Eve Zibart and Bob Sehlinger

The Unofficial Guide to California with Kids, by Colleen Dunn Bates and Susan LaTempa

The Unofficial Guide to Chicago, by Joe Surkiewicz with Bob Sehlinger

The Unofficial Guide to Cruises, by Kay Showker and Bob Sehlinger

The Unofficial Guide to Disneyland, by Bob Sehlinger

The Unofficial Guide to Florida with Kids, by Pam Brandon

The Unofficial Guide to the Great Smoky and Blue Ridge Region, by Bob Sehlinger and Joe Surkiewicz

The Unofficial Guide to Las Vegas, by Bob Sehlinger

The Unofficial Guide to Miami and the Keys, by Bob Sehlinger and Joe Surkiewicz

The Unofficial Guide to New Orleans, by Eve Zibart and Bob Sehlinger

The Unofficial Guide to New York City, by Eve Zibart and Bob Sehlinger with Jim Leff

The Unofficial Guide to San Francisco, by Joe Surkiewicz and Bob Sehlinger with Richard Sterling

The Unofficial Guide to Skiing in the West, by Lito Tejada-Flores, Peter Shelton, Seth Masia, and Bob Sehlinger

The Unofficial Guide to Walt Disney World, by Bob Sehlinger

The Unofficial Guide to Walt Disney World with Kids, by Bob Sehlinger

The Unofficial Guide to Washington, D.C., by Bob Sehlinger and Joe Surkiewicz with Eve Zibart

the Unofficial Guide® to Walt Disney World for Grown-Ups

1st Edition

Eve Zibart

Macmillan • USA

Every effort has been made to ensure the accuracy of information throughout this book. Bear in mind, however, that prices, schedules, etc., are constantly changing. Readers should always verify information before making final plans.

Macmillan Travel

Macmillan General Reference USA, Inc.
1633 Broadway
New York, New York 10019-6785

Produced by Menasha Ridge Press

MACMILLAN is a registered trademark of Macmillan General Reference USA, Inc.
UNOFFICIAL GUIDE is a registered trademark of Macmillan General Reference USA, Inc.

ISBN 0-02-863353-9
ISSN 1523-0643
Manufactured in the United States of America
10 9 8 7 6 5 4 3 2 1
First edition

Contents

5 Sports and Recreation

6 Nightlife

7 Adult Education

8 Drinking and Dining

List of Maps

This book is for Tracey and Kevin, in hopes that your Walt Disney World honeymoon is just the beginning of the magic.

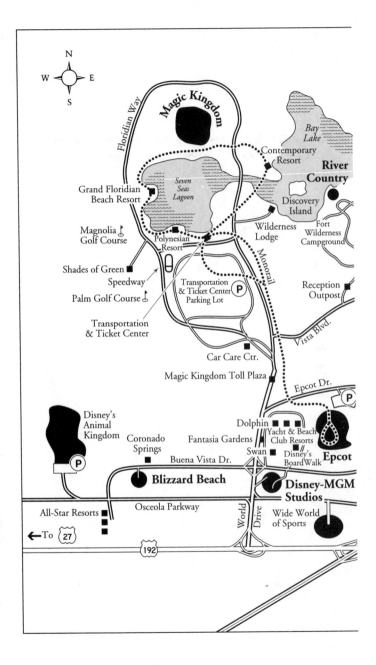

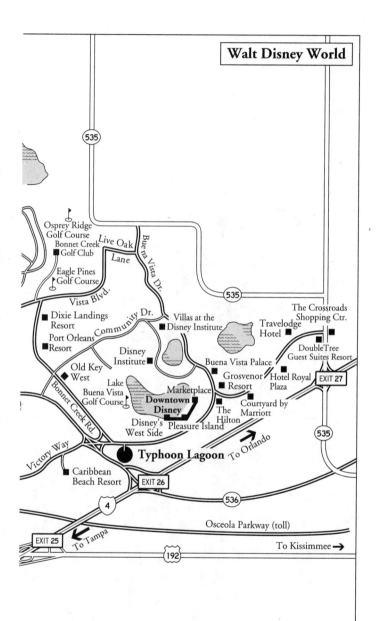

Walt Disney World

535

Osprey Ridge
Golf Course
Bonnet Creek
Golf Club

Live Oak Lane

Buena Vista Dr.

535

The Crossroads
Shopping Ctr.

Eagle Pines
Golf Course

Vista Blvd.

Community Dr.

Villas at the
Disney Institute

Travelodge
Hotel

Dixie Landings
Resort
Port Orleans
Resort

Disney
Institute

DoubleTree
Guest Suites Resort

Buena Vista Palace

EXIT 27

Old Key
West

Lake
Buena Vista
Golf Course

Marketplace

Grosvenor
Resort

Hotel Royal
Plaza

535

**Downtown
Disney**

Courtyard by
Marriott

Bonnet Creek Rd.

Disney's
West Side

Pleasure Island

The
Hilton

Typhoon Lagoon

To Orlando

Victory Way

Caribbean
Beach Resort

EXIT 26

4

536

Osceola Parkway (toll)

EXIT 25

To Tampa

192

To Kissimmee →

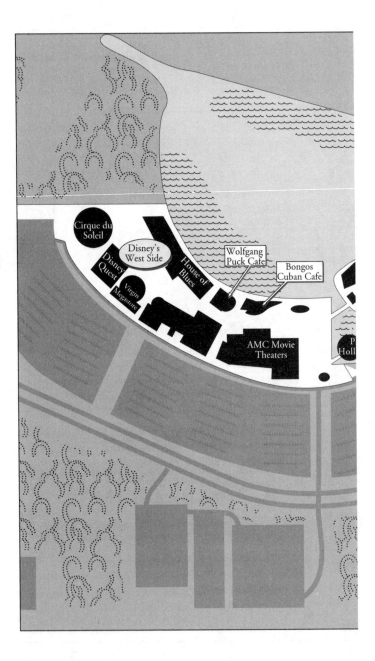

Cirque du Soleil

Disney's West Side

Disney's Quest

Virgin Megastore

House of Blues

Wolfgang Puck Cafe

Bongos Cuban Cafe

AMC Movie Theaters

P
Holl

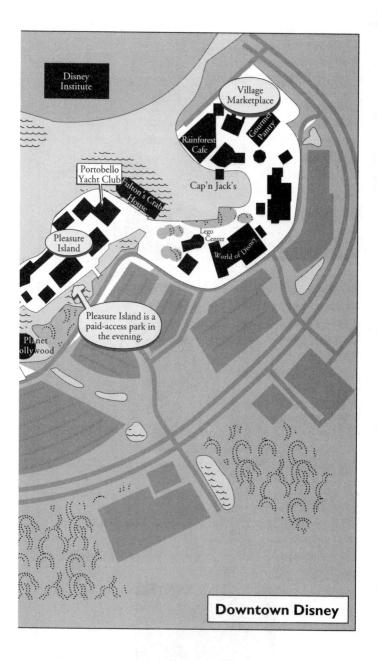

Downtown Disney

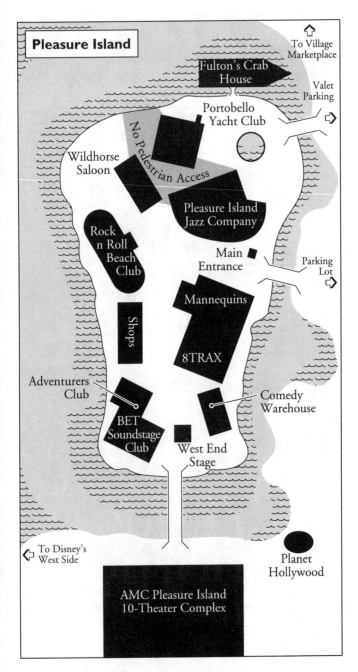

Pleasure Island

To Village Marketplace

Fulton's Crab House

Valet Parking

Portobello Yacht Club

No Pedestrian Access

Wildhorse Saloon

Pleasure Island Jazz Company

Rock n Roll Beach Club

Main Entrance

Parking Lot

Mannequins

Shops

8TRAX

Adventurers Club

Comedy Warehouse

BET Soundstage Club

West End Stage

To Disney's West Side

Planet Hollywood

AMC Pleasure Island 10-Theater Complex

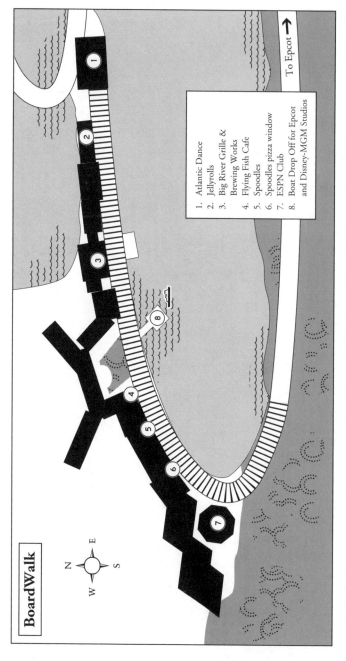

BoardWalk

1. Atlantic Dance
2. Jellyrolls
3. Big River Grille &
   Brewing Works
4. Flying Fish Cafe
5. Spoodles
6. Spoodles pizza window
7. ESPN Club
8. Boat Drop Off for Epcot
   and Disney-MGM Studios

To Epcot →

the Unofficial Guide® to Walt Disney World for Grown-Ups

1st Edition

Introduction

Ladies, Gentlemen, Children of All Ages

Walt Disney World for Grown-Ups is not an oxymoron. Walt himself certainly wouldn't have thought so (not that Walt would have considered himself "grown up"). Every year, nearly 40 million tourists from all around the world travel to Orlando, Florida, to participate in the most successful amusement concept in history: part playground, part schoolroom, and part Sugar Plum Fairy. Many of them bring their children, of course; many have been coming since they themselves were children. But an increasing number of young singles, empty-nesters, professionals, and seniors also flock to Walt Disney World, often for the first time, with as much enthusiasm as any six-year-old alive. In fact, as is obvious from the "graying" of Disney World's workforce (or cast members, as employees are known), it's a powerful draw for reluctant retirees and part-timers.

What these multigenerational visitors all have in common is a lack of self-consciousness, a sense of playfulness, and perhaps also a sense of relief in escaping what seems to be an increasingly dark and complex real world for the instant gratifications of the Magic Kingdom. Other resorts may bill themselves as "antidotes to civilization"; Disney World offers an antidote to incivility; a respite from violence, squalor, hunger, and environmental depredation; and even a sort of inoculation against aging. Like Peter Pan, the international citizens of Disney World never grow up. In many ways, it is Walt Disney's greatest gift, as close to eternal youth as we will ever get. Ponce de Leon may have failed to find his fountain in Florida, but only because he was in the right place at the wrong time.

YOUNG AT HEART

To a great extent, the "character" of Disney World reflects the personality of Walt Disney himself. Even in his 50s, when Walt first started work on the original Disneyland, he was building it as much for himself—for if there was ever a man who cherished his "inner child," it was he—as for his children. It was the settings and stories, the fairy tales and young people's adventures that he remembered from his own childhood, such as *Kidnapped, Tom Sawyer, The Jungle Book,* and *20,000 Leagues Under the Sea,* that Walt re-created in the original Adventureland, Fantasyland, and Tomorrowland.

Cars were still novelties, and the fact that they frequently ran amok at the mercy of primitive wheels and even worse roads may have inspired those early bumper car rides as much as the first true race cars did the Grand Prix track. Buffalo Bill's Wild West Show was a fabulous fixture of Walt's childhood—Buffalo Bill himself, like Disney, was a native of Kansas—and Wyatt Earp, who had spent his early law-enforcement career there as well, was the inspiration for the very earliest silent cowboy films.

When Disney was still a toddler, the Wright brothers made the dream of flight a reality, in a clumsy-winged box far less graceful than Dumbo; when he was in his mid-20s, Charles Lindbergh made the first Atlantic air crossing and inspired the very first Mickey Mouse cartoon. "Plane Crazy," as it was called, wasn't released until after the better-known "Steamboat Willie," but that other alter ego echoed Mark Twain as much as it played on the contemporary popularity of Edna Ferber's *Show Boat* and its Broadway-musical adaptation. In fact, as Walt himself not only scripted Mickey's adventures but also provided his actual voice until 1946, it could plausibly be argued that all of Mickey's roles reenacted Walt's own childhood fantasies.

Because Disney grew up in the age of such inventors as Thomas Edison and Alexander Graham Bell and photographers George Eastman and Eadweard Muybridge, and in a time when the medical research of Walter Reed, Louis Pasteur, and their colleagues seemed to promise a future free of disease, he remained fascinated by and absolutely confident of the advances of science and technology. His original vision for Epcot, the Experimental Prototype Community of Tomorrow, was of the sort of technological utopia that Jules Verne would have welcomed. And for many of the "original" Disney generation—those uncynical and often unsophisticated post–World War II baby boomers who could easily remember iceboxes and water pumps and operater-assisted telephones—the rapid transformation of American culture was just as magical as it seemed to Disney. Even the so-called atomic age was still a phrase to conjure rather than debate.

So, though the actual Epcot is not a living city but a sort of super World Exposition—another beloved concept from Walt's childhood—it nevertheless echoes the unquestioning faith Disney's generation grew up placing in the captains of industry. "Progress equals prosperity" is the credo; dreams, especially the American dream, can come true if you're young at heart.

And the young at heart, like the Super Bowl quarterbacks and the Olympic heroines, go to Walt Disney World, where they are joined in a mini-nation of thousands of their peers. For the 20-somethings who throng to Disney World, the continual barrage of music, lights, lasers, and special effects provide a three-dimensional ambience as stimulating as a computer game. (And, of course, the video and virtual reality games at Disney World are always state of the art.) For the 30- and 40-somethings, the movie references that make up the Disney vocabulary are as familiar as their real-life friends. For the older visitors, the international pavilions of Epcot's World Showcase and the safaris of Animal Kingdom may be as close to foreign travel as they will ever come. For the self-indulgent, a few days at the resorts can supply the delights of three or four holidays at a single booking: beach time, wilderness hiking, club hopping, chore-free dining, sports, and shopping.

None of this is purely coincidental. So broad a potential audience doesn't go unnoticed, or unexploited. Neither does the ever-greater proportion of disposable income and increased leisure time represented by older people. Self-fulfillment is no longer considered selfish, it's spiritual; it may require years to achieve. The Disney corporation is notoriously clever at creating both demand and supply, and over the past decade it has deliberately targeted middle-aged professionals (supplying business services in the hotels and offering management and efficiency seminars to companies), sports fans (purchasing ESPN and constructing the huge ABC Wide World of Sports complex), active retirees (the Disney Institute), and trend-savvy yuppies (expensive restaurants and wine bars). Under CEO Michael Eisner, who uses his own very broad interests as the litmus test for Disney programs, the company has gone from being amenable to all age groups to specifically targeting each age group. The advertising campaigns proclaim, "It's time to remember the magic" and "It's just not the same without the kids." Golf and tennis facilities abound, along with luxurious spa services and ever-more expensive merchandise, not to mention a new cruise line. Seniors are so important to Disney economics that an entire branch of the guest services department is geared to silver-age visitors.

Hence, This Book

So, it's no joke to talk about visiting Walt Disney World as an adult. There are, however, a few concerns that we will try to address in this book to make your visit as pleasant, relaxing, and fulfilling as possible. Questions of health and comfort, volume levels, and handicapped access are certainly relevant; issues of respect for older visitors, safety, and stress are equally important and may affect your choices of accommodations and attractions. We'll also try to remind you of little things you may not have considered, such as what to pack, when to travel so as to get the most fun (and the least competition) out of your trip, what to spend your time on (and what to avoid), and where to go for more information. In fact, you may find that the portions of the book that address what you should do to prepare are bigger than the part dealing with what to prepare for; that's intentional. We say, spend the time now, and enjoy your trip later.

Above all, we promise to be blunt. We are "unofficial" precisely because we don't want to be beholden to anyone or to have to pull our punches. We pay our own way, buy our own meals, walk (or ride) the parks ourselves without being known to the Disney folks. It's not that we don disguises or try to trap cast members into indiscretions; we just want to experience the park exactly the way you will and then give you our honest opinion. If we think a restaurant is overpriced, we'll say so. If we were somewhat disappointed in Ellen's Energy Adventure—and, unlike many other reviewers, we were—we'll tell you why. If we have been annoyed by condescending cutesy-ness, unpleasantly delayed, or made uneasy, we'll say so. And we'll say why, so that whether or not you agree with us, you'll at least understand our reservations.

But we're also pretty tolerant, adventurous, and curious; so if we have been unexpectedly delighted or intrigued, we'll tell you that, too. We share time-saving (and temper-saving) tips, secret hideaways (even though we realize that means our secret is, well, not so secret anymore), and painful experiences, all in hopes of ensuring that your experiences are pleasurable. Unfortunately, we can't prevent rudeness or inconsideration, so we remind you to hold tight to your good humor. That, in fact, is the real key to enjoying your visit.

For the purposes of this book, we will occasionally divide adults into three age groups: younger adults, meaning primarily those in their 20s and 30s; middle-agers, from age 40 heading up toward 60; and seniors or, as they say these days, "silvers." Obviously, these are loose categories; active middle adults may well enjoy the more rigorous thrill rides, and curious seniors frequently find the interactive computer games as fascinating as any youngster. But as a general guide to stamina, comfort, and interest level, these groupings may be helpful.

PROS AND CAVEATS

There are obvious benefits to visiting Walt Disney World without children, starting with the freedom to set your own schedule. (Or not to; improvisation and impulse are pleasures in themselves, especially if you ordinarily live out of an appointment book.) You can go regardless of the school calendar, which immediately suggests you may be able to go cheaper (because big family times are peak rate seasons) and among fewer fellow travelers. You can eat when you want and what you want, without having to make sure there's a hot dog on the menu. You can get up early and take advantage of the park's more quiet hours without having to make sure everybody is dressed and together; conversely, you can stay out as late as you like. You don't have to worry about your party becoming separated, memorizing where to go to be found if they're lost, or losing track of time. You don't need to compromise on the schedule—to ride Dumbo the Flying Elephant in return for touring the greenhouses. You don't have to wonder whether a ride is too scary or too childish for your kid, or whether he or she's ready for the straight but respectful sex education of *The Making of Me*.

You can indulge in unabashed nostalgia if you like, riding through The Haunted Mansion again or walking through the Swiss Family Robinson's treehouse one more time; or head straight to the newest, most realistic rides and sign up for a Disney Institute lecture. You can stand through the 360-degree films in the World Showcase, sit down at the outdoor theaters for the shows, and stop to enjoy the sidewalk performances by the musicians and jugglers.

You can take a personal time-out for a massage, learn (at last) the Lindy, or buy a glass of champagne and stop and smell the roses at Epcot. You can strike up a conversation with one of the international cast members—many of them students, but numerous adults as well—who staff the various pavilions representing their homelands. And since so many of the cast members and greeters are middle-aged or older these days, you can safely ask them about the comfort of a particular attraction. You can interact with the characters as freely as the children (you'd be amazed at how many seniors want to have their photographs taken with Mickey or Mulan or Quasimodo) or stick to the sidelines.

You may even find that you get a whole different set of jokes than children would: For example, the music in DinoLand USA, where the central attractions are casts of dinosaur skeletons and the Countdown to Extinction ride, includes such pun-ishing titles as "I Fall to Pieces," "Bad to the Bone," and "It's the End of the World As We Know It." The mock-theatrical posters in the waiting room of the It's Tough to Be a Bug show feature "Web Side Story," "Barefoot in the Bark," "Beauty and the Bees," "The Grass Menagerie," and "A Cockroach Line." ("Crickets agree—It's a hit!") Restaurants are called things like Copa Banana and Juan and Only's; a street in Port Orleans is called Rue d'Baga.

Walt Disney and his Imagineers shared a prankish, playful humor, which led them to plant visual puns, jokes, and puzzles all over the theme parks as well, such as the fat lady phantom who sings at the very end of The Haunted Mansion ride. "It's not over till . . ." It's sort of the Bullwinkle mentality; you don't have to know why "Boris Badenov" is funny, but it helps. (Especially when you see the tombstone for Paul "Boris" Badenov, one of the voice-over artists who worked for the studio.)

But it is only fair to warn you that there are some drawbacks to traveling child-free. You may find the "fairy dust"—the semi-official Disney term for both the theatrical glitter and the sense of wonder it is supposed to engender among visitors—becomes a little cloying from time to time. (Remember how confused the real-life actor Bob Hoskins was when he entered the animated Toon Town in *Who Framed Roger Rabbit?* That was a Walt Disney film, after all; and you have to wonder whether it wasn't inspired by some Imagineer or cast member's having one too many reality shocks.) You may find the constant volume and bombastic hammering of the ever-present musical background excessive, if not exhausting. And you may not even recognize some of the featured characters who accost you, unless you still make it to every Disney movie opening.

You're almost certain to find the Disney corporation's relentless self-promotion (every movie a parade, every character a T-shirt) awfully heavy-handed; and you may be seriously concerned by the commercialization of Epcot's "adventures" (Exxon presents the Universe of Energy, IBM presents the future of the Internet, Coca-Cola and American Express bring you The American Adventure, and so on). McDonald's is the sole corporate sponsor of DinoLand USA (and all these corporate entities have hidden VIP lounges above and behind their "pet" attractions).

Similarly, you may have a strong and not entirely pleasant reaction to the my-country-love-it-or-leave-it boosterism of The Hall of Presidents or the American Adventure, especially if you are neither white nor male. Or you may wonder about the animal welfare issues that have been raised by the construction of the Animal Kingdom.

Finally, there is the fact that even if you are without kids of your own, you are going to be surrounded by kids, which means that you are still likely to fall victim to a certain number of tantrums, "accidents," arguments, and underfoot hazards, not to mention all those thoughtless or intentionally rude parents trying to scythe you off at the ankles with their strollers. Even when the 6- to 18-year-olds are in school, the preschoolers are not, though again, the weekdays are apt to be safer because their parents are presumably working. So there's no way to have a purely "grown-up" Disney World vacation, if that's what you're looking for, and we would be lying to pretend the title of this book amounts to any such guarantee (although we'll try to help you get away from the kiddie crowd as much as possible).

Nevertheless, you can have a very interesting, educational, relaxing, even transporting vacation, and these days, that alone is some sort of magic.

How to Use This Guide

This book is designed to be chronologically useful, so to speak, in that it begins with advice on advance planning, including what time of year to go; tries to help with deciding where to stay—that is, which of the many resort hotels attract the least children or offer the best amenities—and what to pack and take with you. We'll also tell you a little about the various package vacations and ticket options, and whether they'll actually save you money.

We will address the special needs of disabled visitors (Walt Disney World, as it happens, is unusually hospitable to handicapped and impaired guests) and give a few tips for foreign visitors. We'll try to direct guests who can't quite cut loose from the office to hotels with business services and tell you where to get money and financial services. And we'll tell you when special events such as flower shows and sports championships are scheduled, so that you can enjoy your favorite hobbies as well as the parks.

Then we go into the various parks themselves, the attractions in each you'll most enjoy and the ones you can easily pass up. (As mentioned above, we occasionally describe attractions in terms of age groups, but these categories aren't meant to be restrictive, just indicative.) We'll pick the best of the restaurants, warn you off the worst, and point out some of the little pleasures you might have overlooked. We'll talk about budgeting time, or rather allowing it, as we hope to help you relax rather than get you wound up and overextended. We even evaluate the shopping opportunities and give you our pick of the parks' souvenirs, so you don't have to waste time gathering the goodies for the family unless you want to. (Yes, we know—for some people "vacation" translates as "shop op.")

How Come "Unofficial"?
DECLARATION OF INDEPENDENCE

The author and researchers of this guide specifically and categorically declare that they are and always have been totally independent of the Walt Disney Company, Inc.; of Disneyland, Inc.; of

Walt Disney World, Inc.; and of any and all other members of the Disney corporate family not listed.

The author believes in the wondrous variety, joy, and excitement of the Walt Disney World attractions. At the same time, we recognize that Walt Disney World is a business, with the same profit motivations as businesses the world over. In this guide we represent and serve you, the consumer. If a restaurant serves bad food, or a gift item is overpriced, or a certain ride isn't worth the wait, we can say so, and in the process we hope to make your visit more fun, efficient, and economical.

WHY SO MANY BOOKS?

We've been writing about Walt Disney World for almost 20 years. When we started, Walt Disney World pretty much consisted of just the Magic Kingdom theme park and a few hotels. Since then, Walt Disney World has grown to the size of a city and is equally if not more complex. Our comprehensive *Unofficial Guide to Walt Disney World,* tipping the scales at over 700 pages, still provides the most in-depth and objective coverage of any Walt Disney World guide and is the basic reference work on the subject.

As thorough as we try to make *The Unofficial Guide to Walt Disney World,* there is not sufficient space to share all of the tips and information that may be important and useful to some of our readers. Thus, we have developed four additional Walt Disney World guides, all designed to work in conjunction with what we call "the big book." Each of the four, including this guide for grown-ups, provides specialized information tailored to very specific Walt Disney World visitors. Although some tips from the big book (like arriving at the theme parks early) are echoed or elaborated herein, most of the information is unique and was developed especially for *The Unofficial Guide to Walt Disney World for Grown-Ups.* Just as there's not space in the big book for the grown-up-oriented material presented here, likewise we can't cram all of the detailed information from *The Unofficial Guide to Walt Disney World* into this guide. Rather, the two guides are designed to work together and complement each other.

In addition to *The Unofficial Guide to Walt Disney World,* by Bob Sehlinger (784 pages; $16.95), the following titles are available:

- *Mini-Mickey: The Pocket-Sized Unofficial Guide to Walt Disney World,* by Bob Sehlinger; 320 pages; $10.95

- *Inside Disney: The Incredible Story of Walt Disney World and the Man Behind the Mouse,* by Eve Zibart; 225 pages; $9.95
- *The Unofficial Guide to Walt Disney World with Kids,* by Bob Sehlinger; 224 pages; $9.95
- *Beyond Disney: The Unofficial Guide to Universal, Sea World, and the Best of Central Florida,* by Bob Sehlinger and Amber Morris; 250 pages; $9.95

Mini-Mickey is a nice, portable, *CliffNotes* version of *The Unofficial Guide to Walt Disney World.* Updated annually, it distills information from the comprehensive guide to help short-stay or last-minute visitors quickly decide how to plan their limited hours at Walt Disney World. *Inside Disney* is a behind-the-scenes unauthorized history of Walt Disney World, and it is loaded with all the amazing facts and great stories that we can't squeeze into the big book. *The Unofficial Guide to Walt Disney World with Kids* helps families make the most of their Disney vacation, and *Beyond Disney* is a complete consumer guide to the non-Disney attractions, restaurants, outdoor recreation, and nightlife in Orlando and central Florida. All of the guides are available from Macmillan Travel and at most bookstores.

TALK BACK TO US, PLEASE!

If you have any advice of your own to offer after you visit Walt Disney World or if you'd like to agree or disagree with something we've said, we'd appreciate hearing from you. (Big ears are the symbol of Disney World, after all.) A new twist, a savvy traveler tip, or an anecdote could be helpful for future editions; there is a short questionnaire in the back of this book that we invite you to fill out. (We absolutely will *not* pass your name or address along to any other organization or mailing list; it's for our information only.) Or you can just tell us about your vacation in your own words. You can reach us by writing to the author, Eve Zibart, c/o *The Unofficial Guide to Walt Disney World for Adults,* P.O. Box 43673, Birmingham, AL 35243. If you are a regular Internet user, you might also notice that several of the online bookstore sites have links for reader responses to particular books, but they are usually fairly general in nature.

Part One

Planning Your Visit

When to Go

Visiting most places means taking the weather seasons into account; but Florida is famous as a year-round escape. In fact, that's one of the main factors Walt Disney considered in deciding to build his second Magic Kingdom: the heavenly weather. So, the seasons to consider in this case are more social than climatic: school semesters with their scheduled vacations and holidays; rainy or dry weather; and high- and low-price seasons.

The heaviest crowds are during spring break, particularly Easter week; from May to September; Thanksgiving week; and the fortnight from about December 18 to New Year's Day, which is the most hectic of all. By heavy, we mean prohibitively so—in past years, as many as 100,000 people have been packed into the Magic Kingdom alone. Three-day holidays, such as Presidents' Day or Veterans Day, tend to draw people more heavily than ordinary weekends, too.

The best times to go are in late September or October, when the weather is usually still well into the 80s, the rainy season is passing, and the kids are in school; or in the weeks after Thanksgiving and before Christmas, specifically the early and middle weeks of December. The parks are fully and elaborately decorated for the holidays, there are Santas and storytellers from a dozen different nations and traditions in Epcot, candles and tree lights glitter everywhere, and even the most stolid-looking strangers suddenly put on stocking caps with ears and smile at you. Average temperatures are in the high 60s or low 70s during the day and high 40s to 50s in the evening, but it's usually sunny and nice for strolling. (Both fall and pre-Christmas hotel restaurant reservations tend to be at their loosest.) And though you may be heartily tired of Christmas music after a day or so, it's probably no worse than it would be in your local shopping mall.

January may seem sort of an afterthought, but it can be a good third choice. Sure, the Christmas lights and international Santa characters are gone, the parks' hours are shortened, and a few of the attractions, such as Blizzard Beach and Typhoon Lagoon, may be closed for their annual facelift. But on the other hand, accommodations are still cheaper; even if the parks do open later or close earlier, the lines to get into attractions are so much shorter that you aren't likely to need the extra time. As a resort guest, you can get into at least one major theme park a day by 8 a.m. and stay until 2 a.m. at Pleasure Island. One night, at least, you may be able to stay out late in the Magic Kingdom for only $10 (see "How to Cut Costs," below). It can be cool or even chilly (the averages are 60° during the day and about 45° at night, though it's frequently warmer), but it's generally fairly dry, and there are plenty of indoor activities if not.

As far as days of the week are concerned, Friday, Saturday, and Sunday are nearly always busier than the other four, although Monday holidays are usually bad. Tuesday and Wednesday are nearly always good, and Thursday usually is, too. (Remember that just because school is in session doesn't mean that the under-six-years-old set is under any restrictions; so you're better off going during the week on the theory that at least some of the parents may be at work.)

If you must go in July, you'll probably be able to save some money, because hotel rates are low, parks stay open late, and both Fourth of July and Bastille Day (the French Independence day, July 14) make for lots of fireworks and parades; but be prepared for serious heat, humidity, dehydration, and massive crowds. If you do want to visit during a major holiday or around a special event, such as Christmas, be sure to make your reservations well in advance—as much as a year in some cases, although the next couple of New Year's Eve celebrations are pretty much sold out already—and confirm at least once.

What to Pack

In most cases, packing for a Disney World vacation is pretty simple. Just follow the comfort rule. Shorts, T-shirts or polo shirts, and sweatshirts or sweaters will carry you well into December; a casual dress or reasonably neat pair of khakis will make you look downright respectable. The single most important thing to pack are comfortable shoes—two pairs at least, because wearing the same shoes through and then after hours of walking is a good way to develop sore soles, if not worse. Do not make the teenager's mistake and wear super-heavy high-top athletic shoes that add 10 pounds and 20 degrees to your feet; or sandals that rub between the toes. Or any pair of new anythings on your feet.

If comfortable shoes are the number one priority, the second is clothes with expandable or forgiving waistlines. Even if you don't think you're going to eat much, the scent of food is constantly in the air (some of it intentionally "blown" into the streets, like the candy smell on Main Street in the Magic Kingdom), precisely to spark your appetite. Seasoned travelers know that a change in schedule can cause bloating as well as dehydration, paradoxically, and you don't want to find yourself holding your breath through Body Wars and feeling as if you're wearing two seat belts at once.

Women should abandon purses for waist packs or convertible totes, or even backpacks: There are fashionable and ergonomically designed versions these days, and your shoulders will thank you. Men might want to try waist packs, too, or at least consider thinning out the stuff they carry in their wallets, not so much because of pickpockets, but because some attractions have molded seats or constraints that may make you uncomfortable.

A bathing suit is almost always useful; even in the cooler season, you may want to head for the spa or catch a few rays around the numerous pools. If you plan to play a few rounds or sets, your shorts and T-shirts can probably do double duty. If you really want to save time at the airport or save your arms in transit, you can even leave your golf clubs behind and rent them at the resort, that is, unless you want to play every day. If you don't have a small, lightweight camera, or you would like to have a video record of your trip without investing in a new camcorder, you can rent one at the parks or buy inexpensive disposable flash cameras, which actually do quite well outdoors. And since you can't take flash photos of attractions or much else indoors, anyway, what's the difference? (Disney processors can deliver your photos in two hours; look for signs at all four theme parks or ask at your hotel.)

Of course, if you are doing the romantic thing, getting married or celebrating an anniversary, you may need to dress up. A couple of restaurants—Victoria and Albert's in the Grand Floridian and Arthur's 27 in the Wyndham, for example—require gentlemen to wear at least a jacket (preferably a tie, as well) and women to dress appropriately, although they've been known to bow to ambiguously semi-casual wear. One or two other eateries, such as Wolfgang Puck at Disney's West Side, ask men to wear at least soft collars (that is, polo shirts) rather than T-shirts. However, most restaurants are used to the casual resort look.

As for outerwear, try to get something with dual use. A rain-proof top of some sort is essential any time from May Day to Labor Day, when the heat and humidity mean almost daily showers, however brief. Small fold-up umbrellas are far preferable to the traditional sort, not only because you can stash them in your bag instead of hauling them around but also because a crowd of people wielding pointed implements or leaning them against souvenir counters can be dangerous. (And then there are the ones hung on chair arms that trip you up in the restaurants.) Also remember that you will be moving in and out of air conditioning, so sleeves you can roll up and down or a scarf you can toss around your shoulders (and across the back of your sun-baked neck) may come in handy.

Spring and fall, you'll want a lightweight jacket or a sweater in case a breeze comes up at night or you want to take the ferry instead of the monorail. Something along the lines of a trench coat with zip-in lining or walking coat with a sweater will usually do in winter, though it's smart to have the anti-wind accessories— gloves, earmuffs, hats, or scarves—tucked in your bag for the worst days. And nearly any time of the year, remember to pack sunblock and sunglasses; December sunburns can be just as painful, and may even be exacerbated by windburn.

Just don't overload yourself. Frankly, years of travel (and packing) have convinced us that most people carry more clothes than they really need. As obvious as those easy-packing tips you see in travel magazines may be—pick things that don't wrinkle, pack lots of light layers, and so on—most visitors fill up their suitcases with new outfits for every day. Who are you trying to impress? Plan your packing the way you'd plan everyday life at home—as if you were going to the mall or a movie and were going to be walking all day and climbing in and out of cars and buses. Besides, most people find it difficult to resist buying at least one sweatshirt or souvenir T-shirt while they're visiting Walt Disney World, and then they have even more clothes to carry.

Of course, you should pack any prescription medications you need; but you should also either bring along ackup supply in case you spill, contaminate, or misplace it.   1g along a doctor's prescription for a replacement supply (see "Travelers with Special Needs," below, for pharmacy information). The other traveling "musts" are over-the-counter medications and ointments. People tend to drink more coffee and more cocktails on vacation, so be sure to pack headache medicines, Alka Seltzer, and the like: Hotel shops are famous for marking prices up, and it saves space if you only pack a few packets from your home supply. If you are allergic to bites or stings, remember the antihistamines. For scratches and small annoyances, a small tube of Neosporin or other antibiotic ointment is helpful. Be absolutely sure to pack bandage strips and muscle-pain antidotes as well—blisters can ruin an otherwise wonderful trip.

The number of uses we have found over the years for zippered plastic bags is incredible, from keeping lotions and shampoos well away from clothes to bathing suits or sink-laundered underwear that didn't dry. They also keep silver from tarnishing, which means you can wear a little chain or pin without having to polish it every day in the humidity; they're essential for leftovers, because though the sit-down restaurants may have doggie bags, the bags will come in very handy at the walk-up concessionaires, fruit markets, and carts. They even work as emergency rain hats.

A few other tiny items that have proven extremely useful are packets of disposable stain remover and a handkerchief—an old-fashioned man's handkerchief, not a pretty little showpiece.

Between bad weather, allergies, air conditioning, damp bus seats, and so on, a good 12-inch square of cloth is a lifesaver. Even when crowds are relatively thin, you are apt to be in close contact with a lot of ice cream bars, barbecued turkey legs, cotton candy, fudge, and so on; and one of those towelette-sized spot treatments can save you a lot of heartache and dry-cleaning money. A tiny penlight, either of the sort that hangs on your keychain or even the credit card–sized ones, may come in handy if you are trying to read maps at night or locate an unfamiliar key. Hand sanitizer gel is a good thing to have in your waist pack, especially when lines to the bathroom are long and you just want to wash your hands.

And finally, though there is not a particular crime problem at Walt Disney World—at least not compared to most travel destinations (and remember, it is larger than a lot of cities)—there have been incidents of auto break-ins, pickpockets, and even rare room intrusions; so there is no good reason to walk around flashing a lot of expensive jewelry or worrying about leaving your earring at the pay phone. Leave it at home and stick to the costume stuff, or leave it in the hotel safe except for the big party. That way, even if you lose an earring, you can replace it quickly and cheaply at the next vendor cart. You might be surprised by what nice-looking silver you can find on the street.

Where to Get Information

The problem is not getting information, it's not getting an overload. For one thing, the Walt Disney Company now has not merely its own World Wide Web site but its own portal, à la America Online. The Go network can be used for all the usual Web surfing and shopping, but for your purposes, the place to start is *disney.go.com*. From there you can get accommodation rates, information on booking cruises, restaurant information, and so on, by browsing the links. You can even make your reservations directly through the Web site, if you don't mind giving your credit card number to a computer (not that Disney is any less safe than any other online shopping mall, but you never know).

In addition, almost any travel site on the Web will have at least a fair amount of Disney World data, and so will the usual suspects among travel, such as the American Automobile Association (AAA).

For complete but not exhaustive details on the various hotels, their rooms and rates, and current packages, stop by an American Express office or other travel agency and get the Walt Disney World vacation brochure or call Walt Disney Travel at (800) 327-2996 or (407) 828-3232 and have it mailed to you. (This is not a good bet if you're planning to go within 90 days, however, as it may take several weeks to arrive.) If you already know pretty much about when you want to travel and where you want to stay, you can call the Walt Disney World operators at (407) W-DISNEY (934-7639), set up your vacation, and give them a credit card deposit. You can buy your Park Hopper passes and admission tickets at the same time.

If you are staying in a hotel within Disney World borders (and you probably should, as you'll see in the next chapter), there will be newsletters in your hotel room with current park hours, special events, and so on. A few of the restaurants are much harder to get into than the rest, among them Victoria and Albert's at the Grand Floridian, the American wine–savvy California Grill at the Contemporary, Fulton's Crab House at Pleasure Island, the Coral Reef in the Living Seas pavilion at Epcot, and Arthur's 27 at the Wyndham Palace. There is a special dinner reservations line to book seats as much as two years in advance, though most restaurants cut the list off shorter than that. Call (407) WDW-DINE (939-3463).

The two live-music dinner shows, the Old West–style *Hoop Dee Doo Revue* in Pioneer Hall at Fort Wilderness Resort and the nightly Polynesian Luau on Seven Seas Lagoon at the Polynesian Resort, are also surprisingly popular. Disney World staffers say that the food is better than the entertainment at the *Hoop Dee Doo Revue,* and the entertainment better than the food at the Polynesian Luau; we think, frankly, for $40+ a head, neither is worth the trouble. If you still want to go, you should make reservations as soon as possible. To make reservations at restaurants at the resort hotels once you've arrived, either stop by the guest relations areas in your hotel lobby when you check in or dial directly from your in-house telephone.

How to Cut Costs

One of the best ways to cut costs is to visit when hotel accommodations are the least expensive. You can find bargain rates, though not always at all resort hotels, in January and early February; July; late August until nearly Thanksgiving; and in December until Christmas week. These extra-value periods generally coincide, not surprisingly, with school schedules, when most families aren't free to take vacations, so for those traveling without kids, they are doubly ideal.

Second, if you're planning to fly into Orlando, see if there's an airfare/accommodations package that suits you: Delta is the "official" Walt Disney World airline (call Delta Dream Vacations at (800) 221-6666), but sometimes you'll see other travel packages advertised, or ask your travel agent. American Express is a special friend of the Disney establishment; call (800) 241-1700.

The Magic Kingdom Club gives its members discounts on rates, meals at some restaurants, sports fees, and shopping. A two-year membership is about $65 a person or $75 for a couple; it's $50 a person or $60 for married seniors. If you might go back frequently, it could add up to good savings; call (800) 893-4763. This is an underpublicized perk: Many corporations, credit unions, social organizations, and even the federal government and most state governments have memberships for their employees, so check with your boss.

Other memberships or jobs can be useful as well: See if your hotel offers any AAA or AARP discounts. Active or retired military personnel and their families are entitled to stay at the Shades of Green resort, which is near the golf courses and may be particularly ideal for older vets: Shades guests get discounts on greens fees (up to 50% in value season) and 10% off park admissions; there is shuttle bus transportation to the Transportation and Ticket Center (TTC); and VCRs in each room with a video "vending machine." If the resort is full, there may be some discounted accommodations made available at other Disney hotels. Call directly at (407) 824-3600.

Another way to save money is to figure out just how convenient and/or luxurious you want your accommodations to be. After all, if you're not doing much more than showering and sleeping at your hotel, you don't need turn-down service. If you decide to go for the cheapest room, you can ask about being shifted to a room with a better view when you check in, and it may not cost you anything. But if you're planning a honeymoon, you may want that grand piano. For more on choosing your hotel, see "Part Two: Where to Stay."

Ask about any special packages or promotions, making sure the packages cover what you want to do. For instance, there are holiday packages that include special performances in the pre-Christmas weeks and even packages aimed at golfing fans (see "Part Five: Sports and Recreation"). Sometimes hotels will offer an extra night for free if you stay a certain number of days, just the way rental car companies do.

Consider juggling your dining schedule. Food and drink are among the biggest items on a Disney World vacation, just because there is so much of it to buy. If you're planning to spend the day touring the World Showcase at Epcot, for instance, you'll proba-bly end up at least nibbling several different cuisines, so don't reserve a table for a big dinner that night. Eat a big meal at lunch occasionally; most restaurants have similar portions, but smaller prices during the day. Don't be embarrassed to take doggie bags; if you don't think you'll eat them the next day, ask the front desk about having a mini-refrigerator brought to your room; it costs about $5 a day, but it might save you ten times that. Or put ice in the sink. Don't forget to stuff one of those zipper plastic bags into your pocket before you leave your room, in case you end up buying fruit or an egg roll or the like from a vendor and want to hang on to the leftovers. (Have you seen the size of those bar-becued turkey legs? Four bucks and you're as stuffed as a . . . well, you know.)

You'll save a surprising amount of pocket change if you carry your own water. Keep refilling those plastic bottles, and you'll not only stave off dehydration and take the edge off your appetite but you'll also save about $2 a pop.

Finally, make sure you really want to see everything on the menu, entertainment-wise. The truth is, you cannot see *everything* at Walt Disney World. You can't even see everything really worth seeing, not if you want to enjoy it. Do you absolutely *have* to play a round of golf when you already belong to a country club back home? Must you get a body treatment at the spa? Why pay for tickets to one of the water parks when your hotel has at least one swimming pool and probably several? Why pay to hang around Pleasure Island with the rest of the would-be hipsters when you can stroll Disney's West End or the BoardWalk for only the cost of the occasional cover or cocktail? Make some of your choices now, and the rest will be easier to make later.

Pick Your Park Pass

The final major consideration is admission tickets. Unless you only want to see one or two amusement parks or are only staying for 48 hours, you will almost certainly save money if you purchase one of the multiday or multipark admission passes rather than buy them one at a time. After all, simple admission to the four major parks—the Magic Kingdom, Epcot, Animal Kingdom, and Disney-MGM Studios—is about $50 apiece; tickets to the water parks and Pleasure Island range from about $20 to $30 (the rates tend to creep up a few dollars every year). If you spend the morning at Epcot and decide you want to go to MGM after lunch, you'll have to buy a second set of tickets, and a third for Pleasure Island—already about $130 per person plus tax. Not only that, but if you do the one-park admission ticket at the gate, it's only good for that day; so if you wanted to get back to Epcot to see *IllumiNations* on another day, you'd have to pay again.

Just be sure you don't buy more than you can use. Some people like moving about from park to park, others would rather explore a single theme world in depth. Fast walkers and stimulation freaks will burn through more attractions than would strollers or less practiced adventurers. Even passes that don't expire aren't worthwhile if you'll never use them (or will lose them in the meantime). So consider your options.

Four-Day Park Hopper Passes

Four-Day Hopper Passes allow you to spend one day in each of the big four parks, but only one per day; with tax, they cost about $177. For adults, who will probably get around the complex more rapidly than those with small children and who want to see Pleasure Island, it may not a particularly good buy. These do not ever expire, however, and unused days can be saved for a future visit. Since neither Disney's West Side nor BoardWalk require tickets, you might be able to convince yourself to skip Pleasure Island—especially if you are not a dancing machine.

The Park Hopper Plus Passes or Length-of-Stay Passes

The Park Hopper Plus Passes or Length-of-Stay Passes will get you the furthest. The Length-of-Stay Pass covers the entire complex: the four big parks, the water parks, Pleasure Island, Wide World of Sports, and all Disney World transportation. You can go back and forth between the parks as many times in a single day as you like. However, you must be staying at one of the resort hotels, and you can only purchase the pass for the same number of days, and no fewer, than you are registered for. Also, the passes expire when you leave, and cannot be used in the future. Prices range from about $160 for three days/two nights up to $300 for nine days. (The ten-day pass is a bargain at $325, but you'd have to be a real Walt-head to want to spend that much time in a single stretch.)

We recommend the Park Hopper Plus passes, which also give you access to the entire complex, but do not expire—that is, if you buy a six-day Park Hopper Plus pass, but use only four days' worth, you can bring it with you on another trip and the pass will be valid for two more days, even if ticket prices have increased in the meantime. Park Hopper Plus passes come in five-, six-, or seven-day packages, with costs ranging up to about $300 for adults. As long as you still have one unused day on the pass, and you are within seven days of the time you first used the ticket, you can "upgrade" more cheaply than you can buy a new pass; so, if you originally thought you'd want a day off, but are captivated by the Animal Kingdom, you can add on.

If you plan to spend more than a week or to return within one year, you might want to consider purchasing "passports," as annual passes are called. The basic passport, which gives you entry to the big four parks and free parking for one year, is about $328. The Premium Passport also includes the water parks, Pleasure Island, and so on; it's about $415.

Also, if you buy a multiday pass, you may be able to get what's called an E-Ticket Express, which will allow you to stay in the Magic Kingdom for three hours after its official closing and ride nine of the most popular attractions, including Space Mountain,

Splash Mountain, *Alien Encounter,* the dinner show at *Country Bear Jamboree,* and Pirates of the Caribbean. Note that these special tickets are usually available only during the slow seasons and only once or twice a week. See details in the "Magic Kingdom: Tips and Tales" section of "Part Four: The Big Four." ("E-tickets," incidentally, were what were required for the most elaborate rides back in the days when you bought rolls of admission tickets by "class" of attraction. The simplest open-air attractions required A- or B-tickets, and were the cheapest; Es were the premium tickets, and the most expensive. Hence when astronaut Sally Ride, a California native who grew up on Disneyland, called her space adventure "an E-ticket ride," she was saying "Wow!" in Walt-speak.)

Admission passes are available at the theme park gates, at the resorts and Disney Village Hotel Plaza properties, and the TTC at the monorail stop outside the Magic Kingdom. However, you may purchase any of the multiday tickets in advance using a credit card, which will save you time in line and will also protect you against later price hikes. Buy them when you make your hotel reservations by calling (407) 824-4321. (You can use a check or money order, too, but it may be slower: send attention Ticket Mail Order, Walt Disney World, Box 10030, Lake Buena Vista, FL 32830-0030.) If you live in a city with an official Disney store, you can purchase passes there, too.

Finally, there is what's called the World of Recreation plan, which adds about $35 a day to your costs and covers some, but not all, recreational fees. If you're the outdoor type, you may want to ask which sports are being bundled at the time you reserve your room, and also what limitations there are (for instance, can you keep the sailboat all day?). Incidentally, if you do plan to play golf, it wouldn't hurt to reserve your tee times well in advance, either—not only will it save you time on the phone once you arrive but you can assure yourself of an early round that won't cut into your theme park schedule. Resort guests are permitted to reserve up to 60 days in advance; call (407) WDW-GOLF (939-4653).

Money Matters

American Express has a special relationship with Disney, and that means they have a special relationship with you, Walt Disney World visitor. There are American Express business service offices in the Contemporary Hotel and just outside the main gates at Epcot.

American Express is also the "official" credit card of Walt Disney World, but MasterCard and Visa work just as well. You may charge meals, souvenirs, spa services, greens fees, and so on to your hotel account if you have already left a credit card imprint at check-in and are carrying your resort ID card. If you prefer to use cash, that's not a problem, either: there are ATMs all over the parks and in most of the resort hotels, as well as full-service Sun Trust Bank branches on Main Street in the Magic Kingdom and across from the Disney Village Marketplace.

The Disney company also promotes what it calls Disney Dollars, which are just what they sound like: imitation money. They are not bonus coupons, in that they do not have any more value than real dollars; and in fact they have an insidious psychological effect—because they do look like play money, people tend to spend them with less care than they would using real greenbacks or even credit cards (although, as we all know, plastic money can seem deceptively "cheap," too) or forget and use them as memo pads and bookmarks. If you don't spend all the Disney dollars, you have to exchange them before you leave or eat the leftovers. We do not recommend that you purchase them.

Travelers with Special Needs

The Disney people have been working for a long time to make the parks handicapped-friendly, even if not absolutely everything can be made accessible. If you use a wheelchair, for example, you and the rest of your party are nearly always allowed to bypass the crowds by using special gates at the monorail, trains, and so on. Many, but not all, resort buses are equipped with wheelchair lifts.

Rest rooms are accessible, and most restaurants are as well. Every resort hotel has at least some accessible guest rooms. Each park has wheelchairs and/or miniature electric carts for rent (a refundable deposit is required), and your rental receipt is good for the whole day, meaning you can elect to leave your wheelchair as you leave one park, ride the monorail, and then get another chair without paying twice. Ferries are accessible as well.

There are Braille guidebooks and maps of the parks available, some closed captioning, and some signed theatrical performances every day. You can arrange for an interpreter to accompany you to a theme park if you call a week ahead. In fact, following an agreement between Disney and the Justice Department, the company has been adding sign-language interpreters, captioning systems, audiotaped tours, and other audiovisual aids at rides and shows; ask cast members for assistance. The maps of each theme park also have symbols that warn you where or at which attractions you may have to transfer in and out of your wheelchair or cart or can't use at all.

All Disney parking lots have specially marked handicapped parking areas. In addition, there is at least one TDD phone for the hearing impaired at the Guest Relations office outside all the major theme parks, also marked by symbols on the park maps; most of the pay phones have optional volume controls (and a wheelchair-height phone as well). There is a whole booklet of information for visitors with impaired sight, hearing, or mobility; call Disney World Information at (407) 939-7807 (TTY (407) 939-7670), or pick up them up at Guest Relations when you rent wheelchairs.

(There has been increasing debate about the use of wheelchairs and electric carts, because some people do grab them in order to take advantage of the shortcuts available to chair users or out of simple laziness. If you do see someone using a chair for pushing packages, or jumping in and out when they don't think Disney employees are watching, you can either report it to a nearby greeter or just make your disapproval known.)

Visitors with various other sorts of injuries, such as neck or back problems, or those prone to vertigo or motion sickness, should heed the posted warnings at the more physically challenging rides such as Star Tours, Countdown to Extinction, Test Track, Twilight Zone Tower of Terror, and Body Wars. Or ask the cast members; in some cases, they may suggest you sit in the middle of a car instead of the front, and so on.

If you are allergy-sensitive, watch out for spring; after all, if you think about it, Walt Disney World is one of the largest cultivated gardens around. Smoking is prohibited inside any building, dining area, or waiting area, by which they mean the queues at attractions; and also most shops, buses, monorail, and ferry boats. But smoking is not banned along the streets, at open-air cafes or garden spots, bars, swimming pools, and so on.

There are first aid stations in each of the big four parks: next to the Crystal Palace in the Main Street area of the Magic Kingdom; in the Odyssey Center on the left as you move from Epcot toward the World Showcase; in the Guest Relations building at Disney-MGM Studios; and near the base of the Tree of Life at the Animal Kingdom. If you have a medical emergency, doctors are on call for 24-hour service; dial 911, contact the hotel operator for assistance, or call Sandlake Hospital (phone (407) 351-8550).

If you lose your prescription medication, HouseMed (phone (407) 239-1195) or Turner Drugs (phone (407) 828-8125) will get you a refill and have it delivered to your hotel, but you will probably need your doctor's phone number for confirmation. Diabetics should ask to have their insulin placed in refrigeration at resort hotels.

Finally, those with special dietary requirements, including medical restrictions and kosher or vegetarian needs, can dine at most of the table-service restaurants with 24 hours advance notice.

INTERNATIONAL TRAVELERS

All that visitors from the United Kingdom and Japan need to enter the United States is a valid passport, not a visa; Canadian citizens can get by with proof of residence only. Citizens of other countries must have a passport, good for at least six months beyond the projected end of the visit; and a tourist visa as well, available from any U.S. consulate. Contact consular officials for application forms; some airlines and travel agents may also have forms available.

If you take prescription drugs containing narcotics or require injection by syringe, be sure to get a doctor's signed prescription and instructions. Also check with the local consulate to see whether travelers from your country are currently required to have any inoculations; there are no set requirements to enter the United States, but if there has been any sort of epidemic in your homeland, there may be temporary restrictions.

If you need to exchange foreign currency, you can either do so at the airport or wait until you get to Walt Disney World. You may exchange money at the American Express offices outside the main Epcot entrance and in the lobby of the Contemporary Resort hotels; or at the Sun Trust Bank branches located on Main Street in the Magic Kingdom or across the street from the Disney Village Marketplace.

The dollar is the basic unit of American monetary exchange, and the entire system is decimal. The smaller sums are represented by coins. One hundred "cents" (or pennies, as the one-cent coin is known) equal one dollar; five cents is a nickel (20 nickels to a dollar), the ten-cent coin is called a dime (ten dimes to a dollar), and the 25-cent coin is called a quarter (four to a dollar). Beginning with one dollar, money is in currency bills (although there are some one-dollar coins around as well). Bills come in $1, $2 (rare), $5, $10, $20, $50, $100, $500, and so on, although you are unlikely to want to carry more than a few hundred dollars at a time. Stick to $20s for taxicabs and such; drivers rarely make change for anything larger.

American Express is the "official" credit card of Walt Disney World, although Visa (also known as BarclayCard in Britain) and MasterCard (Access in Britain, Eurocard in Western Europe, or Chargex in Canada) are also accepted.

Guide maps to the theme parks are available in French, German, Portuguese, Japanese, Spanish, and Italian. Foreign language assistance is available at most Guest Relations offices (at Epcot's World Showcase, of course, there are native speakers at every "nation"). Some menus, especially at the nicer restaurants, are available in other languages. To arrange for an interpreter, call (407) 824-7900.

Incidentally, some foreign visitors may be surprised to discover that smoking is prohibited in most buildings and restaurants throughout Walt Disney World; be sure to observe all signs, listen to announcements, or ask cast members whether smoking is permitted before lighting up.

A Calendar of Special Events

You don't really need to pick a "holiday" by the calendar at Walt Disney World, even if you are a parade freak. With a half-dozen parades, mini-concerts, light and laser shows, and fireworks displays every day, you'd be hard pressed to avoid one. But if you want a little extra fun, and like to party with several thousand of your closest friends, you might consider either St. Patrick's Day, which is, of course, especially popular on Pleasure Island; or Halloween, a personal favorite, when as many visitors as cast members get in costume, the various chefs seem to compete for jack-o-lantern honors, and there are parties and special dinners all around. As we noted before, you can enjoy most of the Christmas fun, including the four million lights of the Osborne Brothers Christmas display at Disney-MGM Studios, candlelight processions, holiday menus, and even special Santa Mickey (et al.) merchandise for a lot less money and with a lot fewer companions in the weeks before the day itself.

Walt Disney World also hosts a increasing number of pro and high-level amateur sporting events every year (they are one of the reasons the corporation constructed the huge Wide World of Sports complex) and some intriguing exhibitions and holiday celebrations as well. Following are their approximate dates; if any interest you, contact the Walt Disney World reservations folks for specific days. These are not necessarily for Disney World visitors only, so ask if the event requires tickets and try to arrange to purchase them with your passes or other advance orders; otherwise you may find yourself locked out. Or ask about sports events packages by calling (407) 939-7810.

Daily parade times are listed in the in-house publications, on the daily schedule boards within the parks themselves, or you can call the central telephone bank from your hotel room.

Incidentally, although we don't have space to mention most of them in this book, there are also several interesting festivals and events in the greater Orlando area, such as the spring Shakespeare Festival and performances by the Orlando Philharmonic Orchestra; if you are interested in other events, contact the Orlando/Orange County Convention and Visitors Bureau at (407) 363-5871.

January

Walt Disney World Marathon   (Early January) This full, 26.2-mile race each year follows a different track through the various theme parks (although some participants have complained it's more back roads than amusement views) with crowds of early-morning supporters and even costumed characters. A two-day sports expo is part of the warm-up; for information and registration call the Walt Disney World Sportsline at (407) 363-6600.

LPGA HealthSouth Championship   (Mid-January) Since 1995, this has been the opening round for the female pros, held on the Lake Buena Vista course. A two-day pro-am serves as warm-up; call (407) WDW-GOLF (939-4653).

The "Indy 200" at Walt Disney World   (Late January) Indy Racing League competition opens for the year as drivers rev up real, not model, race cars at the 1.1-mile tri-oval speedway near the Magic Kingdom. Race-day tickets $50–125; three-day tickets covering trials and race also available. Call (800) 822-4639 for advance tickets or ask at the TTC.

February

Spring Training   (Mid-February) The Atlanta Braves open spring training at the double-decker stadium in Disney's Wide World of Sports with a 16-game Grapefruit League schedule.

Mardi Gras   (February or March) Another party night at Pleasure Island, with jazz and Cajun and Creole food; now even rowdier with the opening of the House of Blues at Disney's West End.

March

St. Patrick's Day Parade   (March 17) Pleasure Island. Be there, be seen, be green (and the morning after, you just might be).

Easter Parade   (Late March to mid-April) The Magic Kingdom's Main Street turns into Fifth Avenue for a day, with a huge parade, huge crowds, plenty of TV cameras, and late hours.

April

Epcot International Flower & Garden Festival   (Mid-April through May) Topiaries, roses (10,000 bushes of them), specialty gardens, and arrangements, plus behind-the-scenes tours, lectures, and demonstrations.

U.S. Men's Clay Court Championship   (Mid–late April) Top-ranked tennis players in both singles and doubles competitions kick off the American clay-court season at the Wide World of Sports; call (407) 939-1597 or (407) 363-6600.

June

Gay and Lesbian Day   (First weekend in June) This unofficial holiday, which is held not Memorial Day weekend but the first one after that, is actually about a four-day event, which attracts an estimated 60,000 gay and lesbian visitors. Call Good Times Tours at (800) 528-8479 or email info@gayday.com.

July

Independence Day   (July 4) As you would expect, fireworks, flags, and patriotic bands, but also huge crowds and hellacious temperatures.

August

Animation Celebration   (August–September) At the Disney-MGM Studios, already remarkably open to view, you can get even closer to the artists, take a few informal classes, and rub elbows with the characters.

September

Disneyana   (around Labor Day) The Disney fanatics' convention-to-end-all-conventions, this combination seminar, expo, flea market, trivia super-pursuit, and family reunion is only at Walt Disney World on the even years (odd years, it's at Disneyland in Anaheim).

Sports Legend Fantasy Camp   (late September) Still think you can hit that major-league screwball? Civilians put on baseball uniforms at Wide World of Sports.

Epcot Food and Wine Festival   (September or October) The already food-heavy World Showcase turns into a real movable feast with cooking demonstrations, guest chefs, wines by the glass, taste tests, and so on.

October

Soap Opera Festival   (Early October) If you only have "One Life to Live," you'd better spend at least one weekend of it here, where you can see those soap heroes and heroines up close, quiz the writers, and slam the doors on a few familiar sets. Of course, since Disney owns ABC, you're only going to run into the casts of that network's serials, but since they're among the most popular, you'll be plenty busy.

Babe Ruth Baseball Blast   (Mid-October) The ultimate at-bat for mid-teen players at the Disney Wide World of Sports.

Pleasure Island Jazz Fest   (Mid-October) With the Pleasure Island Jazz Company as headquarters, some big names in the jazz biz pick up the nighttime slack (and watch for a few surprise guests over at Jellyrolls on the BoardWalk).

Walt Disney World/Oldsmobile Golf Classic   (Mid-October) Disney World's Magnolia, Palm, and Lake Buena Vista courses draw some of the top names in golf for a $1.5 million purse; call (407) 824-2250. The Classic Club Pro-Am, held concurrently, is open to all Gold Classic Club members (annual fee, $5,000) brave enough to tee up with the pros.

Mickey's Not-So-Scary Halloween Party and Parade   (October 31) Which Wicked Witch is walking with you? Watch out!

November

Festival of the Masters   (Mid-November) A huge art exposition and sale, including some fairly established names, at the Disney Village Marketplace.

Disney's Magical Holidays   (Thanksgiving through New Year's) The Christmas lights go up, the candlelight processions begin, concerts warm up, the trees are lit every night (the Osborne Family's Spectacle of Lights in MGM Studios has four million lights by itself), characters put on special holiday dinner shows, and the prices are right. Storytellers fill Epcot, fireworks go holiday-ish. Our pick of the seasons.

December

Harlem Globetrotters (Christmas–New Year's) The home stand for America's longtime dunking champs at the Wide World of Sports. Call Ticketmaster at (407) 839-3900.

New Year's Eve (December 31) Epcot's World Showcase, the Magic Kingdom, Pleasure Island, Disney-MGM Studios, and BoardWalk all host special parties and fireworks, along with several of the resort hotels.

Part Two

Where to Stay

Location, location, location. That's a realtors' joke, but it does apply to some extent to your vacation planning as well. But it's only one factor. Others involve your own vacation style: balancing quiet with amenities, privacy with convenience, atmosphere with cost.

You can pretty much customize a Walt Disney World vacation according to your preferences. Is this a romantic getaway? (If so, stop here and cut to "Part Three: Romance in 'the World'," for a full rundown of the most romantic hotels.) Would you rather fend for yourselves or be waited on hand and foot? Are you more interested in teeing off or taking tea? Cutting roses or cutting the rug? Working out or working in your room? Or—back to location— is proximity to particular theme parks or recreation facilities your primary concern?

This is far from a complete rundown of every hotel or resort in the area; if you would prefer to consider every option, then get the advance planning brochures or books mentioned in Part One. The "big daddy" of this series, *The Unofficial Guide to Walt Disney World,* has hotel ratings that take into account everything from leaking light to carpet fittings, reading lights to refrigerators. But we have tried to pick out a few of the hotels with special qualities we think adults will enjoy most, whether luxurious or lean; so if you are content to simplify your choices and to get the flavor of various resorts, read on.

Note that some of the hotels we mention are not true Disney resorts, but are called "partner hotels"—located within Walt Disney World, but owned and operated by outside companies.

However, since you can make reservations for them through the Disney system and guests there enjoy the same privileges as resort guests, we have included them where appropriate.

GENERAL TIPS

Wherever you are thinking of making reservations, ask about special packages or rates; you never know when you might get a break. Mention any memberships or travel club discounts. Active and retired military personnel have their own resort, Shades of Green. See "Part One: Planning Your Visit" for more information.

And keep asking: Unless you sound as though you are ready to commit right there and then, or at least know roughly when you're traveling, operators are often reluctant to talk rates. But be polite, and be persistent.

When you make reservations at a particular hotel, ask precisely what in-room amenities are provided: All have alarm clock/radios and voice mail, for example; but not all have hair dryers, which many business travelers may have come to take for granted. (If you come up short a dryer or iron, call housekeeping; they generally have some.) Some have minibars; if not, all have small refrigerators for rent.

If you are handicapped, ask about accessible rooms, available in all resorts; but also ask about monorail access; the Contemporary Resort Hotel has a monorail stop inside, but the station, which was one of the first constructed, is not wheelchair accessible. Every resort hotel also has nonsmoking accommodations available.

Keep in mind that check-in time at Disney hotels is not until 3 p.m. (1 p.m. at the Fort Wilderness campsite, 4 p.m. at Old Key West and the Villas at the Disney Institute), so either take a later flight or be prepared to kill a little time. Check-out is 11 a.m.

If you can't leave home without your pet, your choice is simple: the Fort Wilderness campgrounds. That's it. There are day kennels outside the four theme parks, so your critters can be cared for while you cavort, but no overnight options. Disney has too many animals of its own to risk infection or confrontation.

Unless you're only staying a couple of days, have rooms at one of the hotels with its own Monorail station and only want to see the Magic Kingdom and Epcot, you will probably wish you had a car. The intraresort bus system is impressive, but it can be slow—

particularly after about 8 p.m., when you may find yourself sitting on a bus stop bench for close to an hour waiting to get back to your own hotel, then having to stop at several other resorts first. The ferries and various other transport options are fun; but they can be cool at night. From the more distant resorts, you'll likely have to transfer at least once from buses to monorail, ferry to bus, and so on, to get to the various attractions. And if you have a dinner reservation or want to see fireworks at a particular time, you'll have to add on a surprising amount of travel time. (Even the dinner reservations clerks remind you to make extra time to get around the park.)

Parking, which is usually $5 a day, is free for resort guests anywhere in Disney World; in fact, if you tell the parking gate attendant at a resort hotel that you have reservations for the restaurant there, you can usually get in anyway—something that may come in handy if you are staying outside the park. However, if you're used to the vagaries of public transport, you can certainly make do without a car.

SHOULD YOU BUY A PACKAGE?

Yes, no, and maybe. Sometimes the packages offer you more than you need. For example, if you are staying at the Disney Institute and taking cooking classes, you will discover that each class involves making a meal, not just watching a chef; and then sitting down to consume it. If you have purchased the plan that included meals, you'll either burst, or you just won't be able to take advantage of it. (Not only that, but many of those class meals will provide you a doggy bag's worth as well.)

Some packages emphasize the recreation facilities of certain resorts, and that implies that the user fees are included. But have those charges spelled out before you agree; most of the time you'll have to pay the same greens and rental fees as nonguests.

Sometimes the real bargain packages are sold out—another good reason to make your reservations as far in advance as possible and to go off-season. There actually are some four-day, three-night packages that include length-of-stay passes for two adults that start at about $600. These don't include Pleasure Island or the water parks, but you might decide you don't really need them.

Instead, consider a dip in your hotel's various waters and then a night of entertainment by Cirque du Soleil, far and away the classiest theatrical performance in the World; dinner at Fulton's Crab House, and some live music at House of Blues (house bands free, special guests may require tickets). You might even get in a late movie at the 24-theater AMC. These are all at Disney's West End, which, unlike Pleasure Island, is open to the public.

If you are celebrating or honeymooning, you may want to go whole hog; in that case, ask about those packages and review "Part Three: Romance in 'the World'." But remember, you can plan all those little special outings yourself, and probably for less; who needs an in-suite violinist when you can eat at Tony's Town Square Restaurant in the Magic Kingdom and play *Lady and the Tramp* yourselves?

SHOULD YOU STAY OUTSIDE WALT DISNEY WORLD?

The short answer to that is no. There are too many fringe benefits to being a guest of Walt Disney, Inc.—some smallish, admittedly, but they do add up.

The transportation is free and a lot quicker if you don't have to first shuttle or drive from outside. Parking is free for Disney guests, too, so you can elect to shorten your travel time if you like going without paying the $5 daily tab. You are eligible for early admission to at least one major park every day, giving you at least a half-hour's lead, and sometimes more, over the general public. You have guaranteed admission at any time, so that even if the parks are closed by overcrowding to the general public, you can still get in. You have discounts on recreational fees and can make many reservations simply by punching numbers on your bedside telephone. And there's always express check-out, which can save you another long queue, especially if you have a plane to catch.

You can charge meals and purchases to your hotel room if you're carrying your room ID (although the usual credit cards will do just as well). Occasionally having your ID also gets you a discount, like the ones on admission to the 24-cinema AMC Theatres in the West End—that is, if you're planning to spend your vacation watching movies. One really nice benefit of being a resort guest is that when you buy merchandise, you can arrange to have it either taken to the park's front entrance, so you don't have to schlep it around all day; or even delivered all the way to your hotel room. There is certainly a sense of community, artificial or not, that envelops you while you're within the boundaries of Disney World.

However, if you have stayed at the various resorts before or just can't get exactly the reservation you want, we would recommend (and again, we're not trying to be comprehensive here) the Hyatt Regency Grand Cypress for luxury accommodations and lots of amenities. Its facilities almost equal Disney World's: five restaurants (including the local chic fave Hemingway's) plus 24-hour room service, a million-dollar art collection, spa and health club, tennis (a dozen courts in all, five lighted), racquetball, 45 holes of golf (including an 18-hole PGA course), an equestrian center, and a 21-acre lake with various non-motor boats. (The only question is, why ride over to Disney World at all?) Rooms and villas start at about $200 and work up to about $1,500; call (407) 239-1234.

If you are one of those who champion Donald Duck over Mickey Mouse—or your significant other does—you might want to check into another first-class property, the Peabody Hotel, which, like its Memphis parent hotel, makes duck-watching almost a worship service. Every morning at 11 a.m., the resident ducks parade out of their rooftop hutch to their own private elevator, down into the atrium, and across a red carpet to the marble fountain; at 5 p.m., they reverse and march out. As in Memphis, the formal restaurant is called Dux, but none are served—either as customers or as entrees. The hotel also boasts four lighted tennis courts, personal trainers in the fitness center, TV sets in the bathroom (you didn't want to miss the market closings, did you?), and one of the area's best wine cellars. Of course, the hotel paraphernalia is duck-y. Rooms start at about $250 and go up to about $1,500; call (800) 732-2639 or (407) 352-4000.

For those who prefer the B&B life, Perri House, only about ten minutes away, but quite a mindset beyond the borders of Disney World, is a small (six rooms, each with private bath) but extremely attractive bed and breakfast that has its own pool and spa and extensive grounds ideal for bird-watchers. Call (800) 780-4830 or email perrihse@iag.net.

Resorts in "the World"

FIRST CLASS ALL THE WAY

The Walt Disney World Swan and Dolphin resorts were not designed by Disney Imagineers, though you might certainly think they were. They were the playgrounds of postmodern architect Michael Graves; in fact, they are not Disney-owned properties at all, though guests have all the perks. These are our personal favorites, primarily because they are smartly staffed, patronized by business types and savvy travelers rather than families, and because the style tends more to the surrealistic rather than to the stridently whimsical. Not only that, they are among the most strategically located for adult travelers, balancing accessibility and quiet. See "Part Three: Romance in 'the World' " for a full description of the Swan and Dolphin hotels.

One of the more obviously luxurious resorts is the Grand Floridian, also described in Part Three; and it does have a lot to offer: a white sand beach, a spa and fitness center, elaborate theatrical dining, and so on. But the tone strikes some people as rather hoity-toity; the music in the lobby can be disconcertingly loud, and the complex is frequently crowded with sight-seers, a surprising number of families with small (loud) children, and plantation nostalgics waving fat cigars. (Disney has put out a contract to have the Grand Floridian entirely renovated, but it is not expected to look obviously different.)

Instead, consider the Yacht Club Resort: It has a breezy, Nantucket/Cape Cod atmosphere with its own lighthouse and boardwalks, lots of polished wood, and burnished brass (and boxes of chess or checkers pieces available for your room on request). It, too, has its own mini-water park, Stormalong Bay, with a white sand beach and marina; offers an unusual number of sports facilities, such as croquet and volleyball, plus fitness rooms, sauna, massage, and so on. Some of the recreational facilities are geared to the younger crowd—the main pool has a pirate ship, lighthouse, tanning lagoons, and so on—but it has a very adult-conscious staff; in fact, while the Grand Floridian was ranked 49th in *Travel & Leisure*'s Top 100 hotels in the world, the Yacht Club ranked 22nd, and 13th among resorts in the United States. And it generally runs about $50 a night less than the Grand Floridian.

Like the nearby Swan and Dolphin resorts, the Yacht Club has easy walking access to Epcot and the BoardWalk, and it has a water launch directly to MGM Studios. The monorail makes it easy to get to the Magic Kingdom, and the bus service to the Animal Kingdom and Blizzard Beach is fairly swift. Its major drawback is that it also attracts a fair amount of families with small kids, but going off-season and asking for an upper-level room usually solves that problem. (Its sibling resort, the Beach Club, shares most of the facilities but is a little sportier, more casual in atmosphere, a few dollars cheaper—and is apt to house even more kids.)

If you really want to go first-class, you can opt for the concierge-service rooms at the Yacht Club, where the tab (varying with the season, but around $300) includes continental breakfast and afternoon snacks, wine or cocktails and hors d'oeuvres in the evenings, and 24-hour room service.

At the Villas at the Disney Institute, choices range from town houses to treehouses to quite large and very expensive suites (up to $1,200 a night). The treehouses, circular (actually octagonal) natural-wood structures that are elevated on stilts, make for great romantic hideouts; but because they have three bedrooms, they're fairly expensive at $375–400 a night. (Of course, if you are traveling with another couple, it could be fine.)

Although open to all, the Villas are better bets for those actually "enrolling" in Disney Institute classes because they are fairly remote from the theme parks. (Happily, this means that the population is generally in their 30s and older.) Health club- and spa-lovers will be in heaven here; Institute staffers speak ayurvedic and stay on the cutting edge of wellness. Golfers will like the facilities, too—a pro shop, putting green, and driving range as well as a full PGA course right on site—so mixed-interest couples should check it out. There are refrigerators and coffeemakers in all, full kitchens in the largest suites. Remember, if you're taking many cooking courses at the Institute, you don't need to purchase prepaid meal packages, because these are not only hands-on but hands-in kitchen lessons.

LATE-NIGHTERS' NEST

If you are a night owl, and expect to stay late at Pleasure Island and Disney's West End, you may prefer to be over in one of the

Hotel Plaza resorts so you don't have to wait for a bus late at night. (Obviously you can drive from your resort hotel, or take a taxi, but our recommendation means a clear head and extra cash.) The nicest and closest is the Wyndham, formerly the Buena Vista Palace; a multitower complex that is privately owned but accepts reservations through the Disney World operators (call (407) 939-7639). This is the site of one of the best restaurants in the resort area—the elegant, rooftop Arthur's 27—and the romantic favorite Top of the Palace lounge, which offers patrons a free champagne toast at sunset and a view of *IllumiNations* a little later. (It also houses the Laughing Kookaburra bar, with 80 brands of beer and the sort of live entertainment that suggests.) The Wyndham offers a very large full-service spa and innovative fitness center (water aerobics and so on), recreation facilities including lighted tennis courts and a sand volleyball court, three pools, and its own private lagoon. Rooms range from $200–250. Very nearly as nice, and with a few particular attractions of its own, is the Hotel Royal Plaza a few doors away; see the description under "Bangs for the Bucks," below.

Next to the Wyndham is the Grosvenor Resort, also independently owned (it's actually a Best Western—check your travel clubs); it's not terribly showy, but is quite comfortable and has plenty of recreation and spa facilities. And its Sherlock Holmes–themed Baskerville's restaurant is the site of popular murder mystery dinners on weekends, so if you've always wondered about the curious incident of the dog in the night—the one that didn't bark—you might love this.

Your other late-night friendly facilities are the BoardWalk Villas and BoardWalk Inn. These have a lot to offer in terms of entertainment, in that the ESPN Club, Jellyrolls and Atlantic Dance clubs, the carnival midway, and street performers are all literally at your feet. But think about what that will mean when you're ready to call it quits: The sound can come right up through the building. Odd lights are glaring at all hours. Not only that, but both resorts are popular family attractions, heavily trafficked by teenagers and children who may not be able to get into the nightclubs, but who therefore are likely to get up long before you do. It's not cheap, either—rooms go for $200–300. As a somewhat quieter alternative, see the description of the Yacht Club above.

THE SPORTING LIFE

The Contemporary Resort is not, perhaps, the most atmospheric of the hotels. Even though it long since shed its 1950s neo-Aztec/Tex-Mex decor, and a mariachi band no longer plays through the afternoon, some of that rec-room style lingers in the orange furnishings, the mosaic in the atrium, and, of course, the pyramid structure itself. Nevertheless, it has six lighted tennis courts, a marina that rents out sailboats of various sizes—you have to be at least 18, which helps limit the traffic a little—and offers parasailing and water skiing. You may luck into a promotional rate of less than $225, but it would, as we said, be luck.

As described in the next chapter, "Part Three: Romance in 'the World'," the Dolphin Resort has 24-hour tennis play, a state-of-the-art Body by Jake fitness center, and lots of whirlpools; it's also walking distance to the Fantasia mini-golf course. If outdoor sports and some version of camping (from tents to log cabins) are your passion, read the description of Fort Wilderness below.

And no, the All-Star Sports Resort is not for the sports enthusiasts, only for the sports spectator. Aside from a swimming pool, it's strictly commercial sponsorship. And it's positively a child magnet.

BANGS FOR THE BUCKS

The Caribbean Beach Resort was Disney World's first budget resort—rooms are about $125 a night—and has seven pools of its own, a beach and marina, mini-bars in the rooms, and even its own miniature version of Discovery Island, called Parrot Cay, complete with old Spanish Main ruins and bridges. It does attract a lot of kids in high season, but if staying at your own hotel and hanging around the swimming pool isn't what you had in mind for your vacation anyway, you probably won't care. Restaurant choices are reminiscent of a major shopping mall: a food court with counter-service restaurants, or the Captain's Table, your basic American prime rib grill. Ask for a room in Trinidad South, which is the farthest from the lobby and has its own beach.

A little-publicized but highly hospitable hotel is the Hotel Royal Plaza, where standard rooms start at about $110 and deluxe rooms—those with in-room whirlpools—are only about $150. And that's before the discounts that the Hotel Royal Plaza accepts for members of AAA and other travel clubs. If you can get a premium room with a view toward Pleasure Island, you can watch the fireworks there from the privacy of your own balcony—or maybe even the whirlpool. Talk about bangs for the buck!

The Hotel Royal Plaza is sort of Caribbean-lite in style, though not with great conviction; but the rooms have mini-bars and safes, hair dryers, coffeemakers, VCRs and a video library, and even videocamera rentals for those suddenly inspired. (Nope, no more "bang" jokes, even if this is an adult vacation.) For more traditional fun, there is a swimming pool and sauna, a public whirlpool for those who stick to the budget, and a smallish fitness center. You can walk over to Downtown Disney, which pretty much sets you free to party late and walk it off; there is also bus transportation from the hotel to the major parks.

If camping is one of your hobbies, you can rough it in beautiful territory at Fort Wilderness for as little as $35 per campsite; either set up a tent and use the rest rooms, showers, and laundromat down the lane; or borrow your parents' RV. You can even do most of your own cooking, as most visitors here do (there are two markets); and this becomes the absolute rock-bottom Disney World vacation.

Fort Wilderness is ideal for nature lovers: You can walk (or bike) to River Country and take a water launch to Discovery Island. For the less active, there are also electric carts for rent. There are pools, a marina and beach, a lot of outdoor games, fishing and canoeing, even tennis and horseback riding. If you really get into the mood, you can sit around the evening campfire and watch a movie in the main building with the other happy campers. And as mentioned above, the campgrounds are the only accommodations that allow you to have pets (not running loose, of course).

Obviously, this draws a lot of families (did we mention the petting farm and the hay rides?) and in hot weather, a lot of bugs and thunderstorms. If you want things a little more comfortable, ask for a full-service hookup and get water, electricity, an outdoor grill, sanitary disposal, and even a cable TV hookup. If you want super privacy but even more amenities, rent one of the trailer homes or prefab log cabins, which get you a full kitchen, housekeeping services, air conditioning, a daily newspaper, voice mail, and, yes, cable TV. It'll cost you from about $200 to $250, but it's pretty much having your cake and eating it, too.

BUSINESS AND PLEASURE

The Swan and Dolphin resorts both have business centers with printing and color printing, fax, and copying services available, plus e-port access, and (from the hotel) video processing. But the number of business conferences here can't disguise the fact that this is platinum-card stuff; see "First Class All the Way," above.

The Contemporary Resort has a convention center and an American Express Travel Services office in the lobby. The Grand Floridian also has a convention center and business services, so after that tiring conference call, which helps you write off this vacation, you can honorably saunter into the luxury spa for a massage.

If you'd like to save a little money, but without giving up services, consider the Coronado Springs Resort, a rich, Old Mexico–style complex with courtyards, fountains, stucco and terra-cotta buildings with a few Mayan ruins here and there, several swimming pools, a mini-water park, another white sand beach, fitness center, salon, and so on. Because it is also used as a convention hotel, it may be ideal for visitors who have to keep in touch with the office: There's an extra phone jack in every room (for portable computers and modems). Coronado Springs has particularly good access to the Animal Kingdom and Blizzard Beach. Rooms start at about $125.

Part Three

Romance in "the World"

Money can't buy you love, but at Walt Disney World, it can supply just about everything else—champagne, caviar, atmosphere, fireworks, even strolling violins. There are little benches in rose gardens to toast in, romantic rides to hug in, scary rides to clutch in. There are wonderful places for proposing: high in the air of a skycar, adrift in a canoe, strolling through the gardens of China. You can have the ring delivered on a silver platter by a formally attired butler at Victoria and Albert's, say, in the bottom of a crystal goblet. Or perhaps you could arrange to have Mickey act as your surrogate and go down on his knees on your behalf. Write a note from a secret admirer: There's not a bartender or cast member in Disney World who won't act as your accomplice. You can even prove your love in the ultimate style: have the wedding ceremony right in front of Cinderella Castle, complete with fairy-tale coach and prancing white horses (see "And They Lived Happily Ever After," below). Remember, you're *supposed* to fantasize here; go for it.

Many of the romantic possibilities at Walt Disney World are, well, in the eye of the beholder, as we suggest in "Setting the Stage," below. But if you are planning a formal affair or even hoping to stay in one of the resorts' more elaborate suites, make your plans as far in advance as you can, because there is a great deal of competition for the most special rooms. And because the Swan and Dolphin resorts are also popular with upscale business types, their maxi-suites (see "Palaces Under the Seas," below) are much in demand among corporate executives and convention hosts.

Finally, since we're all adults here, let us warn you: Disney World has one of the most extensive safety and security systems imaginable. That means cameras and watchers. Are you following this? There are no attractions, no rides so dark, or nooks so deserted that you can safely demonstrate your devotion. Cast members are fully conversant with the X-rated activities of fans of Pirates of the Caribbean—more conversant than you have any desire to know. The underwear collection from Space Mountain is legendary. Some of these in-house videos have even made it—anonymously, of course—onto the Internet, and these days, that's no joke. So stick to the script, and limit *l'amour* to your hotel room.

Magic Kingdoms: The Most Romantic Hotels in "the World"

We'll remind you once again: Romance is a big-ticket item in Disney World. After all, it's part of the magic. There are treehouses for overgrown Tinkerbells, verandas that rival Tara, and canopies for little Cinderellas.

But just because this is Walt Disney World doesn't mean the fairy dust gets sprinkled everywhere. Unless you're expecting to spend every weekend for the rest of your life channel-surfing though the sports networks, or already do, you are unlikely to find anything romantic, imaginative, or even convenient about the All-Star Sports Resort. (You won't find any sports celebs hanging around, either.) And even if you are a confessed couch potato, your beloved is apt to fry you if you treat your honeymoon like a "Sports Nite" segment. If you go into withdrawal, sneak into the ESPN Club at the BoardWalk and let it go at that.

Castles in the Sky

There is no question that the most famous romantic resort at Walt Disney World is the Grand Floridian, a throwback to Florida's first land rush, where each room has its own veranda (ask for one overlooking the lagoon), the whirlpool is ringed by rose bushes, and the food presentations are over the top. The whole complex is gilded, brocaded, latticed, dormered, etched, marble-topped, fanned, and chandeliered. There is a luxury spa and some rather expensive sportswear shops. Service is smooth, almost unctuous in a pseudo-nostalgic way, which is one reason the Grand Floridian was ranked No. 49 of *Travel & Leisure* magazine's 100 best hotels in the world in 1998.

Most rooms have two queen-sized beds plus a day bed and armchair; bathrobes, toiletries, hair dryers, and daily newspapers are standard. Rooms with lagoon views, which give you an eyeful of not only the Magic Kingdom fireworks but also the Floating Electrical Pageant, are usually a little more expensive than those with garden views, but if you are getting a package, they may be pretty much the same—at least $300, higher around the holidays.

If you are thinking honeymoon, anniversary, or the like, you may be curious about a package there. One such offering, priced for early June, was a three-night stay for two adults on the concierge level, which offers a few cutesy luxuries (private entrance, valet parking), but includes nearly enough food to make dining out entirely unnecessary: continental breakfast, morning snacks, high tea, hors d'oeuvres and cocktails, and late-night desserts and cordials. Three nights there, plus airfare from New York's La Guardia, a midsize rental car, and two Magic Passes good for all ten parks came in at just under $3,000.

The once-in-a-lifetime suite is the penthouse, which goes for $1,500 a night, but comes equipped with a full bar, a built-in Jacuzzi, a baby grand piano (the pianist is extra), and a glorious view of Cinderella Castle and the fireworks over it.

The penthouse also has continental breakfast, high tea, and hors d'oeuvres served. Like concierge-level guests, you may never need to go out for dinner, but if you do, you can keep to the price-be-damned mode by reserving the chef's table at Victoria and Albert's, where even the ordinary diner has at least two servers ("Victoria," in ruffled apron, and "Albert" in cutaway and black tie) and the prix-fixe dinner is $125. Then, if you aren't already staggering, have a cognac in Mizzner's Lounge.

There is one other sort of "castle in the sky" at Walt Disney World—the Disney Institute's Treehouses, which are literally elevated into the woods and come complete with fully equipped kitchens (or room service), and some of which have views of the bayou. (They also have three bedrooms, so you'll be paying for the extra space—in the $350 range.) This is the perfect hideout for Peter Pan fans.

The Sky Inside the Castle

Now that Adirondack/Yellowstone style is trendy again, you may want to go Ralph Lauren rustic at Wilderness Lodge, with its breathtaking eight-story atrium with skylights, 80-foot stone fireplace, interior waterfalls, totem poles, and even the on-the-hour geyser (which mercifully goes "dormant" between 10 p.m. and 7 a.m.). It has its own beach and bubbling hot springs (by now, you've probably noticed that water is never in short supply at Disney World). There are semi-secluded nooks tucked all around the corridors that look down over the lobby, even semi-private fireplaces with sofas and armchairs. Everywhere you look are carved animals, and, for puzzle-lovers, more hidden Mickeys per square foot than you can stand. (In fact, you may be standing on them. Check the carpet.)

The rooms are furnished in modern Mission style, crossed with Sundance-ish cowhides, leather, and quilts; most have two queen-sized beds, and they start at a relative bargain $175 a night. The Artist Point restaurant, which specializes in Pacific Northwest cuisine (of the smoked-salmon variety, not pan-Asian), is interesting and good—sometimes very good. Try to get a forest-view room on an upper level; you get a view of the fireworks and less lobby noise. (Weak kidneys, be warned: One veteran customer said she and her husband had a courtyard room the first time, and all those watery noises had them going to the bathroom all night.)

There is no official honeymoon suite, but there is at least one room with a whirlpool; ask for No. 7084.

Palaces Under the Seas

Though they're not literally thematic salutes to the Little Mermaid, Ariel would be right at home in either the Swan or Dolphin resorts, where aquatic creatures frolic from top (see the hotels' roofs) to bottom (the grotto pool). The Swan looks like a mermaid's version of Miami Vice: turquoise and coral-colored, with seahorses in the chandeliers, swan-backed benches, and so on. The Dolphin's lobby is a huge circus tent, which should give you a clue right off the bat (though what that means about the Cartier boutique shop isn't clear). The Swan and Dolphin share their own beach on Crescent Lake, which is prime *IllumiNations*-viewing territory, and have lots of nice benches among the hedgerows. And fun as these siblings look, they have a surprisingly low children-to-adults ratio. They also have a high business-meeting quotient, so beware of the occasional tie-loosening karaoke party at Kimonos Restaurant in the Swan or Copa Banana at the Dolphin. (Both have several full-service restaurants, including upscale ethnic choices, and 24-hour room service.)

Amenities include mini-bars and in-room safes, coffeemakers, and, yes, hair dryers, daily newspapers, and pay-per-view movies. The Swan's rooms tend to have queen-size beds, the Dolphin's two doubles, though you can request king beds at both. In fact, if you ask for a corner room with king bed at the Dolphin, you may wind up with dual balconies.

The Dolphin's fitness center is on the cutting edge, including a Body by Jake studio; guests who pay a $5 daily surcharge get a morning paper and use of the facility; the Swan's fitness center is free. They share a lap pool and various other pools with waterfalls or whirlpools, a beach with a volleyball net and boat rentals; and the four tennis courts are lit all night. Not surprisingly, the prices are stiff, starting at $250 a night for standard, $350 for the concierge level, and on up; but AAA membership is worth up to 25% off here, and both hotels have a variety of package deals. (Intriguingly, because they rely so much on business travelers, the summer vacation months that are so busy for most other resorts are slacker here, so low-season rates apply.) Also, the Swan belongs to Westin, the Dolphin to Sheraton; so you might also look into chain promotions.

But that's all standard stuff: Probably the most elaborate fantasy housing in all of Walt Disney World are the presidential suites at the Swan and Dolphin. At the Dolphin, the various two- and three-bedroom apartments are laid out on two levels, with several different seating areas, pianos, kitchens with fully stocked refrigerators and appliances, Jacuzzis, and balconies with nineteenth-floor views that take in not only the nightly fireworks but also "pretty much all of Orlando," sighed one employee (who also said wistfully, "I could live there!"). The in-suite decors are as fantastic as anything the Imagineers could have come up with: One is Santa Fe-style, one Japanese-inspired, and one "classical," as in Greek, complete with columns, busts, and drapery. They cost $2,700 (for two bedrooms) to $3,100 a night.

At the Swan, it is possible to get a one-bedroom version of a presidential suite for only $2,275, although it also has two- and three-bedroom layouts; and the decor choices are a little simpler: contemporary, "oasis" (more veranda than South Seas), and southwestern.

Even if you go for the more ordinary accommodations, there are good reasons to pick these two resorts. As we've mentioned, they attract more of a business crowd, or at least a professional one, and are likely to be light on children. The restaurants are a little less predictable than some: At the Dolphin, Juan and Only's Mexican and Sum Chows pan-Asian both get fairly high marks, and Kimono's Japanese and Palio Italian at the Swan do as well.

But there is also the question of access to the parks: You can easily walk from the Swan and Dolphin to the BoardWalk, so you can party until all hours without waiting for a bus; and there are trams and water taxis to the International Gateway into Epcot's World Showcase (although it's a short and quite pleasant walk all the way). The walkway and the bridges are nice places to see the *IllumiNations* fireworks, and you won't get trampled by the departing crowds heading for the parking lots.

There is also a boat from the BoardWalk landing to Disney-MGM Studios; and since Epcot's monorail hooks you into the Magic Kingdom monorail (via the Transportation and Ticket Center), you can head over there or to dinner at the California Grill in the Contemporary or Victoria and Albert's in the Grand Floridian, the two best restaurants in the World, all without batting a busman's eye.

For those who prefer miniature golf to the PGA version, the new Fantasia Gardens course is also nearby.

Setting the Stage

There are some Disney resorts that might attract you because they re-create particular places. For example, if the two of you have always shared a love of jazz or spent a wonderful weekend in New Orleans, you might be wondering about Port Orleans. Indeed, the setting is the resort's greatest virtue, a maze of wrought iron, atmospheric lighting à la the streetlights of the French Quarter, cobblestones, and a really nice riverside promenade. A Dixieland band plays in the main courtyard; there's often a caricaturist, like those who populate Jackson Square, hanging around; a croquet course is laid out and waiting; the row houses have louvered shutters or French doors, and the rooms have ceiling fans. For Mardi

Gras fans, there's Doubloon Lagoon, the theme swimming pool that looks like a parade float with moat.

A river launch carries guests over to Downtown Disney for even more pseudo Mardi Gras partying at Pleasure Island. Port Orleans is also one of the least expensive properties; rooms range from about $100–135. This does mean, though, that while the exteriors are pretty nice, the interiors are less inspiring. Still, if you plan to be out most of the day and then stroll home at night along the "river," you may be very happy here. Ask for a king-size bed and a river view, then spend the extra cash on dinner.

Similarly, although the new Coronado Springs Resort was intended to serve convention traffic, it is something of a bargain ($135 and up), and is really very handsome: a mix of Old Mexican village stucco, neo-Spanish Empire terra cotta and big beams, and elaborate landscaping. Even the mini-water park follows the theme—a Mayan pyramid in a pool. The Ranchos section is the most fan-flutteringly romantic, with its fountains and courtyards; it is also convenient to the fitness center, marina and beach, whirlpool, and so on. Ask for a room on the upper floors. If you have become addicted to the new Southwest chili-grilly cuisine, you'll like the Maya Grill: pumpkin-seed-coated snapper with molé sauce, lots of elaborate desserts, and a South American wine list. Although Coronado Springs is a little remote from the original parks, it's more convenient to Animal Kingdom, so if that's your main interest, by all means, *vamanos*.

Parrotheads will find the closest thing to Margaritaville this side of Key West at, where else, the Old Key West Resort. It is a little remote (which means nice long walks together) and has its own lighthouse, plus several swimming pools, a large whirlpool, and surprisingly large, tin-roofed peach and aqua and seawater-colored villas with balconies and picket fences so cute you'll want to organize a Tennessee Williams cocktail party. Olivia's Cafe makes real key lime pie. And if you can get a studio—which despite its name comes with two queen-size beds, a wet bar, refrigerator, and microwave—you'll really feel as if you've crashed in Jimmy Buffett's living room.

The problem is that this is a Disney Vacation Club timeshare resort, so the less expensive rooms (and even the studios are at least $225 a night) can be hard to get. The good news is that most timeshares are in demand when kids aren't in school, so again, if you can travel off-season, you may be in luck. One-bedroom villas not only add a second sleeping area (king-size beds in the master bedrooms) but also full kitchens, dining rooms, washers and dryers, VCRs, and whirlpools; so for about $300, two couples can live it up very happily. (There are two- and three-bedroom villas, but those get into serious money.)

South Seas and Sailor's Warnings

For many people, the concept of the Polynesian Resort is extremely romantic: lei-sy days in your own South Seas Island paradise, with friendly natives, lush tropical plants and falling water, drinks in funny glasses with paper umbrellas and lots of fruit, cute egg roll appetizers, and pretty girls hula-ing in grass skirts . . . But in fact, it's more like the Marx Brothers' vision of *Cocoanuts* than Margaret Mead's. The resort is getting old—it was one of the first built—and it's starting to look it. Rest rooms in the main building need help badly, the restaurant seems a little tawdry, and the tiki room-ish bar is decorated with hanging TVs instead of orchids. The nightly luau down on the beach is pretty hokey, and the all-you-can-eat 'Ohana restaurant inside is like a cross between those old sweet-and-sour grass huts and the newer Brazilian churrascarias. And they want $300 a night?

If you must stay there (if you had promised her Tahiti and backed out), ask to stay in Samoa, which is the farthest from the lobby; or consider the all-suite Bali Hai, which has a concierge lobby with great views of both the nightly fireworks from the Magic Kingdom and the Floating Electrical Pageant.

Still, if the island lifestyle is what you crave, why not try Caribbean Beach, where rooms start at only $100 or so? If you specify accommodations in Trinidad South, which has a private beach and hopefully fewer children around, you might have more money to spend on those little gifts and flourishes.

"That's Amore": The Most Romantic Restaurants

As with where you stay, what you find romantic in a restaurant may depend on where you're pretending to be. And if you're really in love, you may not have much of an appetite, anyway. But here are a few suggestions for dining in romantic circumstances and with more dependable service.

Victoria and Albert's   Sometimes called V&A's for short, this is Walt Disney World's most expensive and elaborate restaurant, though not, admittedly, particularly avant garde. It's a very fine continental restaurant with classical tastes, a prix-fixe menu, an optional series of wines chosen (very ably) by the sommelier and chef to complement the foods or your own choice from the superlative list. If you happen not to like one of the wines suggested, the sommelier will be happy to consult with you about a replacement. Prepare to spend at least $100 a head here, even if you're not a drinker (although coming here as a teetotaler may be something of a waste), and perhaps as much as twice that, when all tip is told.

The schtick here is that each table has two servers, one man—Albert, in full Victorian houseman's attire; and one woman—Victoria, of course, not in queen's robes but in a maid's outfit that owes as much to 1950s fantasies of Paris past as to any real Victorian-era uniform. Each diner gets a copy of the night's menu with his or her name embossed in gold, like a court proclamation. However cutesy it may be, the service is first-rate. The room is quite lovely, a little pantheon of a place that manages to make every table seem at least semi-private. However, the restaurant is intentionally not large, and there are only two seatings a night, so make your reservations well ahead of time if you can. If you really want to make this special, call even further ahead and try to book the chef's table in the kitchen, where you can actually see all the dinners being prepared. The table sits up to eight people, so a small wedding party (see "And They Lived Happily Ever After," below) could hold a rehearsal-night or even wedding dinner here. And talk about proposal possibilities!

California Grill   One of the best restaurants in the entire area, and one of the few that gets regular customers from Orlando as well as from Walt Disney World, the California Grill is located on the rooftop level of the Contemporary Resort. It has modern food, much of it first-rate; an exhibition kitchen, sushi bar, wood-fired pizza oven, and a great all-American wine list, from which you can order anything by the glass as well as by the bottle. (Note to sushi connoisseurs: Like all the "sushi bars" in Disney World, this has a fairly limited variety, and they don't like to make any substitutions unless you are actually allergic to something.) One way to make dinner here even more romantic is to make your reservation well in advance and make sure you show up early ("priority seating" is a nice way of saying first-come, first-seated). Ask for a window table. If you can't get a dinner reservation, go to the bar or sushi bar. Just before the fireworks are launched over the Magic Kingdom, right across Bay Lake from the restaurant, the overhead lights are dimmed so that the effect is heightened—a really nice way to start the evening. Make sure to check in advance what time the fireworks are, that is, when the Magic Kingdom closes; in the off-season, for instance, that might be as early as 6 p.m. on weekdays, so you'd want to be in by 5:30. On weekends, the fireworks may not show until 9 p.m., so try for 7:30 or 8 and be prepared to wait for the right table.

Artist Point   Also beautifully situated for viewing the evening fireworks is Artist Point at the Wilderness Lodge, which has double windows, wrought iron chandeliers, great murals of the Pacific Northwest, and a salmon/game/grill-heavy menu to match, plus wines from the hot new regions of Oregon and Washington. It's not as cutting-edge as some of the others, but direct and often quite good.

Arthur's 27   Perched atop the Wyndham Palace, Arthur's 27 is another popular gourmet getaway for locals, also a bit pricey but with a great wine list (probably the area's largest cellar, especially of French wines), and with four-, five-, and six-course prix-fixe options that, like Victoria and Albert's, come with wine recommendations. Here, you also have a possibility of great views, especially if you get a private booth that looks out toward the Disney Marketplace and Pleasure Island (though the actual fireworks aren't until later). Start at the Top of the Palace lounge, where you get a free glass of champagne at sunset and maybe another glass from that same wine list, and then mosey on in to dinner.

In terms of backdrop, many people like the huge living wall of sea creatures that passes as decor in the Coral Reef restaurant at Epcot's Living Seas pavilion, and indeed the food is pretty good. On the other hand, it's a little strange to be eating the first cousin of the guy floating by.

In addition, several lounges have at least one romantic corner or a loveseat. There's one in the Ale & Compass Lounge at the Yacht Club Resort. The Stone Crab bar at Fulton's Crab House outside Pleasure Island (no entrance fee required) opens onto a little deck that has a lovely view of the sunset; the bar itself and the bartenders are equally attractive, and the wine list is surprisingly good. If you happen to catch it at a quiet moment, the Tabu Bar in the Harambee marketplace area of Animal Kingdom has a nice view down the "river," and there are Asian vistas across the bridge. Don't forget the tuckaway seatings around the Wilderness Lodge mezzanine. Mizzner's on the second floor of the Grand Floridian has a gentleman's club luxury about it—lots of gleaming mahogany, decanters, and big crystal port goblets—but it's occasionally smoky and/or loud.

"And They Lived Happily Ever After": Weddings and Honeymoons

Mickey and Minnie, the Lion King and his queen, Sleeping Beauty and her prince, Cinderella and her prince, Snow White and her prince, Beauty and her Beastly prince, Ariel and her prince, Mulan and . . . see a pattern here? You, too, can be a prince, or a lion, or even a mouse—whatever your wedding fantasy is, this is surely the place to make it come true. Nor will you be alone: More than 1,700 weddings take place here every year. And forget Niagara Falls: Walt Disney World is the number one honeymoon destination in the world. Generations of little girls who dreamed of being awakened to a new life by a kiss come as close here as they ever will. And don't think we're kidding about the mouse: Both brides and grooms have been known to wear ears under veils and instead of hats. It could even pass for a yarmulke. You can buy special Minnie-ear veils and Mickey-ear top hats in the hat shops, if the urge hits you.

Although the fairy-tale setting is the most famous, you can commission Disney World's wedding team to re-create a fantasy involving any of the theme parks; so if you picture yourselves as Bogie and Bacall, you could do it at MGM Studios, play Tarzan and Jane at the Animal Kingdom, or perhaps dance like Americans in Paris in Epcot. The Disney consultants can also arrange weddings in any of the resorts, so you could go native at the

Polynesian or nice and nautical at the Yacht Club, which has a gazebo in the garden—you name it.

For formal or at least more traditional romantic weddings, Disney's Wedding Pavilion, a Victorian summerhouse near the Grand Floridian beach with a view of Cinderella Castle beyond the altar—and the fireworks, if you like—is the favorite site. Seating 250, it's pure neo-nostalgia the way only Disney could offer it: shiny, fragrant, and guaranteed to draw oohs and ahhs. And it has a smaller photo-ready flower garden, also with a good view of the castle, out in the gardens for the intimate vows. (The Wyndham in the Hotel Plaza also has two wedding gazebos with cascading waters; the Hyatt Regency Grand Cypress has a garden gazebo, too.)

The smaller weddings, called Destination Weddings, are designed for parties of 20 people or so, and can be held in any of the resorts, but not in the theme parks. If you want a private ceremony, referred to here as an "intimate wedding," Disney will arrange an officiate, a honeymoon suite, and theme park passes for a mere $3,000 or so. For any of these arrangements, contact the wedding office at (407) 827-3400, and do it well in advance—like a year. Remember, this is a busy place.

Of course, many of the hotels have honeymoon suites and special packages; call (800) 828-0228 for suggestions.

Here's a fairly recent option: the honeymoon cruise package. Now that Disney has its own cruise line and luxury liners, the *Disney Magic* and the *Disney Wonder,* you can get married at Cinderella Castle, spend a few days exploring Walt Disney World, and then be transported to Port Canaveral for a three- or four-day cruise and a little honeymoon package—a champagne hamper— of your own. The seven-day Land & Sea Odyssey package (which doesn't include the actual wedding) starts at about $1,800 per couple. For a little more, you can get a bigger gift basket, passes to play golf, a Planet Hollywood T-shirt, a massage, and so on.

These are for standard staterooms, however; if you want to get a royal suite with veranda, of course, it will cost you somewhat more. And if you decide to book a week's cruise apart from your customized fantasy wedding and reception . . . and there's airfare . . . well, as Tinkerbell would say, the sky's the limit. On the other hand, you could just get married by a clerk of court and get on board.

Note that AAA members get 20% off cruise rates, which is more than worth the cost of a membership if you don't already have one. For more on the Disney cruises, see "Love Boats: Disney Cruises," below.

The Price of a Princess

The absolutely most elaborate weddings, including the ones where the bride rides in Cinderella's coach and the bridegroom rides (is led, actually) to the castle courtyard on a white steed, and their matching receptions, are customized by Disney consultants at a cost of about $17,500 and more. If you'd like a fireworks display, add another $15,000. The average is about $35,000, though some hit six digits. That's a pricey fairy godmother, but certainly makes for an unforgettable day, or night, as the case may be. Most of the big weddings are performed after hours, though occasionally you'll get to witness the grand procession down Main Street.

THE LITTLE THINGS

There are a lot of semi-secrets about getting good views of the nightly fireworks without having to reserve a penthouse, like the ones mentioned above about the California Grill and Arthur's 27.

Here's a secret place where you can enjoy not one but two such night flight shows. As you step off the water taxis at the Magic Kingdom landing, facing the park entrance, there is a brick walkway along the shore off to your left, in front of and below the monorail station. It leads to a small white sand beach that looks across toward the Contemporary Hotel. Depending again on the time of year and the fireworks schedule (in this case, you want the 9 p.m. show), you could watch the Magic Kingdom's "Fantasy in the Sky" fireworks (they might be slightly obscured by the trees, but not badly) and then only minutes later get a good view of the Floating Electrical Pageant—King Neptune and friends cruising about to Handel's "Water Music"—as it circles Seven Seas Lagoon. Take a bottle of wine or even a picnic with you, but note that you can't take the picnic into the theme park.

In fact, you can't take a picnic into any of the four theme parks, though the water parks are okay (no glass, of course). Depending on the season, you might be able to pack cocktails and hors d'oeuvres and sail out into the water from the Marketplace Marina, enjoy the view with your loved one, and get back before dark.

Here are some other possibilities: Go to the French pavilion at Epcot and get a couple of glasses of champagne (Mumm's Cordon Rouge), which are delivered in flute-shaped plastic glasses. There's a little boulangerie and patisserie there where you can get a little croissant sandwich or cheese and pâte if you like, or you can just settle back on a bench in the back garden and pretend to be in Paris. If you're really careful, you can carry your glasses back to the British pavilion (yes, I know it's treason) and retreat to the even less-trafficked garden behind the shops. You can buy a whole bottle of the Mumm's, and theoretically you could open it, but they really frown on the glass thing, and I can't blame them.

There's also a nice gourmet shop with wines in the Italian pavilion; since several of the Italian "performers" are living statues, this is often a relatively quiet spot to take a break. Although the Matsu No Ma sushi bar in the Japan pavilion is busy at rush hour, you can often find a quiet spot at midafternoon with a view of the temple and gardens (and entertainers) and enjoy some sake without much company.

And if the *Arabian Nights* are among your favorite stories, head straight for the Moroccan pavilion to catch the belly dancer and the surprisingly good dinner. This is also a great place to shop, with embroidered long tunics and matching pants like the ones Pier 1 Imports made famous, only much nicer, for $120; lovely pottery, fine leather and weavings, and even carpets. In fact, this is one of the great secret finds in the entire World: They have an acrobatic troupe that entertains in the courtyard in the afternoon and really good bastela and surprisingly good couscous in the restaurant, which is an even better bargain for early-bird diners who can then stroll around a little more until *IllumiNations* time.

If you need roses at the last minute, like the guy who suddenly decided to propose in the middle of the Polynesian bar, call the Walt Disney World florists at (407) 827-3505 between 8 a.m. and 5:30 p.m. or Gooding's Florists in the Crossroads at (407) 827-1206; they deliver to all the resort hotels.

And here's a little tip that might make your day: Unless you are staying in a hotel right over a restaurant, make sure you have water, juice, screwdriver makings, champagne, fruit, croissants, wrapped-up chocolate desserts—*something* for the next morning, whatever your style—in the room every night. It can be a long walk to the restaurant; besides, very little is more romantic than breakfast in bed.

LOVE BOATS: DISNEY CRUISES

Disney's two show boats, the *Magic* and the *Wonder,* were among the only Disney productions in history to be delayed, but the reasons seem obvious: Nearly 1,000 feet long and 11 passenger decks high, carrying 2,400 passengers, and with three-quarters of their 875 staterooms with ocean views (nearly a third with private verandas), they are hugely impressive ships—inspired, at Disney president Michael Eisner's direction, by the great oceanliners of the 1930s and 1940s.

Although these are, like all Disney enterprises, designed to be family-friendly, the ships are somewhat segregated, and there is an entire deck devoted to children's activities, with programs aimed from age three to mid-teens and a staff of 40 to keep them busy—they even have their own espresso bar. In fact, the Disney folks claim that they have ten times the usual space devoted by cruise ships to children's activities, and you can hope it works.

The ships are, in effect, giant floating Disney Worlds—theme parks with more suntan time. The *Magic,* for example, has a "Beat Street" complex of adults-only nightclubs and lounges that, like a miniature Pleasure Island, samples most of the major music styles; several restaurants including one adults-only establishment called Palo, which has Northern Italian cuisine and great water vistas; a full-sized live musical theater; the Buena Vista Theatre, which shows both classic and more recent Disney films; and another ESPN Skybox for those who can't quite give up the TV screen. There's even a adults-only swimming pool and a full-service spa and salon. (Eisner made a point of not including casinos in the ships because of the family image; however, there have been complaints from so many adults, apparently accustomed to going down to the sea in chips, that he is reportedly considering adding them.)

For all the luxury detail, they are hilariously, unmistakably Disney vehicles, with red, yellow and black stripes, cartoon characters in the trim around the bow, and a 15-foot Goofy hanging upside down painting the ship's name on the stern. As the ship pulls away from the dock, the foghorn plays seven of the most famous notes in musical history: "When you wish upon a star . . ."

The ships depart from Port Canaveral and head to Port Nassau in the Bahamas, where passengers do the usual sight-seeing and souvenir shopping things, and then go on to Disney's own special island, Castaway Cay. (No, there's no name in Disney's lexicon that doesn't refer to some movie or character or other.) There, guests can swim, snorkel, sunbathe—there's an adults-only beach apart from the others—arrange for more massages, dance to the music, or eat throughout the all-day barbecue party.

Again, you could opt for a three- or four-day package during school months, although it won't protect you against families with preschoolers. For more information on Disney cruises, call (407) 566-7000 or go to the Web site, www.disneycruise.com.

Part Four

The Big Four

This is where we get to the good stuff: the theme parks themselves. What to see, what to do, what to stand in line for, and what to skip—by definition, this is one of the most opinionated chapters of this fairly opinionated guide. We're not pulling any punches. We know that there are millions of people out there, *in this same universe,* who find It's a Small World quite charming. In fact, the theme song is rumored to be the most frequently performed song on the planet. And it may well be—although, considering that the phrase "It's a small world, after all" constitutes the entire lyrical product, it probably breaks some sort of Guinness repetition record every day.

But that saccharine little jingle is just one of the reasons this particular attraction gives us the willies. The whole ride is just like a combination doll fashion show and carousel, with those hackneyed ethnic mannequins bobbing up and down on sticks, and that song, which bears a close family resemblance to a schoolyard nyah-nyah-nyah, looping endlessly, deafeningly, brain-damagingly all around you. (Admit it—you can hear it right now, can't you? In fact, you can't get it out of your head.) And since all the dolls have basically the same features, only painted different colors; and all the Asian dolls have pretty much the same eyes . . . well, don't say we didn't warn you. About us *or* it.

Yes, there are rides and attractions at Walt Disney World that are overhyped, juvenile, blatantly commercial, or downright tedious; there are others that, for some visitors, may be too spine-wrenching—even some that may be too exciting. The good news is, there are plenty of attractions that are beautiful, gloriously

Rides Worth Their Wait

The Magic Kingdom:
Alien Encounter
Space Mountain
The Timekeeper
The Haunted Mansion
Splash Mountain
Pirates of the Caribbean
Epcot:
In FutureWorld
    Honey, I Shrunk the Audience
    Body Wars
    Test Track
    The Living Seas
In World Showcase
    China
    France
    Japan
    Morocco
Disney-MGM Studios:
Star Tours
The Twilight Zone Tower of Terror
The Great Movie Ride
The Magic of Disney Animation
Jim Henson's MuppetVision 4D
HorrorLand FunHouse
Animal Kingdom:
Countdown to Extinction
Kali River Rapids
Kilimanjaro Safaris
Pagnani Forest Exploration Trail
Tree of Life
It's Tough to Be a Bug!

gruesome, scary, silly, nostalgic, imaginative, hilarious, or even musically accomplished. Some are, of course, the newest and technically trickiest, but you can't always use the newness of an attraction to gauge its success accurately; sometimes the ones you think you already know about have a few surprises in store. We'll try to keep you from wasting your time on the worst, make sure you see the best, and give measured judgment to the others. If you listen to us, you'll never hear you-know-what again.

The Magic Kingdom

Obviously, this is the children's paradise of the four main parks, but that doesn't mean there isn't a lot worth seeing here. You are a child of the Disney era, aren't you? In fact, you might be a child of several different Disney eras, all represented here, from the nostalgic Carousel of Progress to the very modern Hollywood sci-fi spin-off *Alien Encounter.* Thrill-seekers have made Space Mountain one of the hottest attractions in the entire Disney World complex, but the Magic Kingdom also has several of the most gentle and passive rides for frailer visitors. Maps are available at City Hall; the wheelchair rentals and storage lockers are in the train station.

THE LAYOUT

The Magic Kingdom resembles the sort of curly-headed tree children often draw (or, perhaps, the stick-figure of Little Orphan Annie). You enter by passing under the tree's roots—the arches of the train station—onto Main Street, U.S.A., which is the trunk of the tree. Walk up Main Street to the rose garden and parade circle in front of Cinderella Castle, and you'll see how the various theme areas branch off along bridges (limbs) over the castle moat from this center point into the crown of the tree. Each of the theme areas has its own little cluster of attractions at the end of the branch; you can either pass from one to the other or go back toward the garden and around to the next bridge. Because you can nearly always see the castle spires, you can use it as a compass point or meeting place. (In fact, there are "spires" at four strategic points of the Magic Kingdom map: The elevated train station at the foot, the castle in the center, Big Thunder Mountain at the far left, and Space Mountain to the far right, so there is almost always a landmark somewhere nearby.)

This parade circle is also the spot to plot your schedule if you haven't already decided, or if your time is limited. Look for the Tip Board, which tells you not only what time various theatrical performances will begin but also the estimated waiting time (and Disney staffers have line-estimating down to a science) for the rides and attractions. Every park has a Tip Board, in fact, and is worth checking into; not only are the line warnings fairly accurate—in fact, to avoid disappointment, they usually add a few extra minutes onto the time predicted—but the great majority of rides have introductory distractions: films, jokey exhibits, preliminary stories, and so on.

If you pass under and through Cinderella Castle, you continue, as if into its courtyard, into Fantasyland, where Cinderella's old animated friends—Dumbo, Peter Pan, Alice in Wonderland, and Winnie the Pooh, now joined by the Lion King and the Little Mermaid—can be found. (Such is fame: The old 20,000 Leagues Under the Sea lagoon has been recast as Ariel's Grotto.)

The Americana sections begin to the left of Fantasyland, in more or less chronological order (and, since the United States were settled in a westward direction, in an appropriate geographical pattern as well) as you move counterclockwise: first Liberty Square (with its Yankee Traders shop), Hudson River–style The Haunted Mansion, Bostonian Liberty Tree, and Philadelphian *The Hall of Presidents;* then Frontierland, where the river becomes the Mississippi (Tom Sawyer Island, Mike Fink Keelboats, the Liberty Belle paddle-wheeler, and, at the border between the Midwest and the Wild West, the Diamond Horseshoe Saloon), and the Wild West is represented by the Frontierland Shootin' Gallery, *Country Bear Jamboree,* Big Thunder Mountain Railroad, and Splash Mountain. (Main Street is the Victorian era section of the Magic Kingdom, so if you want to keep the metaphorical flow going, retrace your steps through Frontierland and back around the hub toward the Crystal Palace, which is a copy of the 1851 London Exposition Hall.)

If you stay on the main route, Frontierland gradually fades into Adventureland, which is even farther over the imagined horizon and includes all sorts of "exotic" destinations: Pirates of the Caribbean, Jungle Cruise, and the shipwreck island of the Swiss Family Robinson Treehouse.

If you go up to Fantasyland and turn clockwise instead, you'll pass the entrance walk to Mickey's Toontown Fair, which was something of an afterthought and which is pretty much all kid territory, anyway; the looping Tomorrowland Speedway, and see the last great "mountain" of the Magic Kingdom, the spiraling Space Mountain. From Tomorrowland you pass back across a hub bridge to the rose garden and down Main Street to the exit.

Don't Miss

Whether you opt for the half-circuit route or just wander the whole park in order, there are at least a half-dozen "must-sees" in the Magic Kingdom. Starting from Tomorrowland and moving counterclockwise around the park—which is what you'll probably have to do if you want to get into either *Alien Encounter* or Space Mountain without waiting a long time—we recommend both of those attractions, with these cautions: Space Mountain is one of the fastest and scariest rides in Walt Disney World, lasting about three minutes and including several abrupt turns and plummets, so those with neck or back problems or vertigo should probably skip it. (The stars and galaxies are pretty good.)

Alien Encounter is just what it sounds like—a monster movie turned fairly grim theatrical experience. Disney CEO Michael Eisner had it shut down before it officially opened and made even scarier; "riders" are strapped into their seats, so the faint of heart or nightmare prone may want to pass on this, too. (No physical shock is involved, however, and it's wheelchair-accessible.) It's not a pretty sight. Great special effects, though. If you like the *Alien* films, you'll love this. (There are some in jokes here, too: The company that is supposedly in charge of the teleportation system is called X-S Tech, which is a pretty valid comment on the ride itself. After all, nothing exceeds like excess. Also note that the robot in the waiting area isn't a real robot—that is, it isn't an Audio-Animatronic, which the Alien is—but a sort of doll robot. Only in Disney World could you have so many subcategories of artificial life.)

Both of these attractions involve sudden blackouts, as do many thrill rides at Disney World; those who suffer from claustrophobia, tend to panic in the dark, or have vision problems with extremes of light and darkness, should avoid these two attractions and be sure to ask the cast members at other rides whether darkness will be a problem.

Absolutely no one of any age should miss *The Timekeeper,* part stomach-churning Circle-Vision 360 special effects film with lovely soaring views of the Earth and beyond (you can always grab the bar or close your eyes for a moment) and part hilarious Audio-Animatronic presentation, with Robin Williams as the voice of the swift-talking Timekeeper robot and Rhea Perlman as the hapless 9-Eye, a sort of 3D flying camera. It's also classic Disney inventor worship, with Jeremy Irons as H. G. Wells and Michel Piccoli as Jules Verne. The one drawback is that you have to stand through the 20-minute show (you can sit in your wheelchair, of course), and those with stiff necks may have to be a little careful not to get whiplash. But this is a stunner.

Don't let the apparent childishness of the old-fashioned The Haunted Mansion put you off: This is one of the best attractions in the Magic Kingdom (and in fact, one that seems to get a few new twists each year). It takes less than 10 minutes, preshow included, but you may have to do it twice—it's jam-packed with visual puns, special effects, Hidden Mickeys (see Part Nine: "Hidden Mickeys" and Other Grown-Up Games, for an explanation), and really lovely Victorian-spooky sets. It's not scary, except in the sweetest of ways, but it will remind you of the days before ghost stories gave way to slasher flicks. This is an easy ride in physical terms, though you have to traverse a moving sidewalk to get into your car, which can be tricky for slow walkers or cane users.

Of the three big "mountain" rides in the Magic Kingdom— Space Mountain, Big Thunder Mountain Railroad, and Splash Mountain—the latter is, oddly, the sweetest and the scariest. That is, the flume cars are said to approach speeds of 40 miles per hour, much faster than the other two; but its *Song of the South* setting and huge Audio-Animatronic animal cast (more than 100 characters) give it a much more elaborate appeal. The apparently sheer drop, which is clearly visible to all comers and will either whet your adrenaline appetite or scare you off, is actually about 50 feet down at a 45-degree angle. That's the only real shock point; but, again, it may jolt those with serious neck or back problems. Nearly all riders will get splashed to some degree when the flume drops. Those in the front row of each "log" will get pretty thoroughly swamped, so be careful what you wear.

Despite its age, and a few stereotypes that remain annoying despite some recent political correction, Pirates of the Caribbean is still a delight; rollicking, simple, with nice special effects, but nothing frightening. It will remind you of a dozen buccaneering movies and books of your childhood, or should. (One could wish there were a jerk chicken concession attached.) Wheelchair users will have to get out of their chairs, but the transition into the "boat" is not too difficult; though there are a few drops that are supposed to indicate water rapids, they aren't rough.

Second Best

This category is a tricky one, of course, because many people will find the Carousel of Progress more fun than *Alien Encounter;* and others will prefer the *Country Bear Jamboree* to The Haunted Mansion. All of these are worth seeing if possible; but we're trying to limit the "Don't Miss" category in order to guide those who may have only a few hours in a single park, may be more effects-oriented than nostalgic, have health problems, and so on. Also, because the Magic Kingdom is the oldest park, some of its attractions have been superseded or updated to some degree in other parks, as is true of *The Hall of Presidents* (upstaged by the *American Adventure* in Epcot).

Starting back in Tomorrowland: Walt Disney's Carousel of Progress is a good-humored look at how invention and technology have improved everyday life; it certainly reflects Walt's personal faith in science, but it also serves as a metaphor for Tomorrowland itself because the "future" in the show keeps working its way into the past. Even though it's been updated, it still seems a little old-fashioned. And it has another of those horrible repeating songs. But it's pleasant, a good sit-down respite (it's wheelchair-accessible), shock- and scare-free, and a treasure trove of Hidden Mickeys.

Buzz Lightyear's Space Ranger Spin is surprisingly sweet; if you ever enjoyed those early video games (they seem so innocent now) where you blasted space rocks apart with your "laser gun," you'll enjoy this. Not much in the way of bumps or jarring, and you can stay in your wheelchair if you want.

Most adults without children will be satisfied just walking through Fantasyland, but there are a couple of stops worth making. Surprisingly fun—if you're not embarrassed to be seen getting in a "kiddie ride" (though it's not)—is Peter Pan's Flight, with its glorious swooping view of old London and Pirates' Lagoon from the "air." Cinderella's Golden Carrousel is a classic merry-go-round with beautiful antique animals; almost everyone will smile on this one. And *The Legend of the Lion King* is very nice, though this is only a super-puppet version, whereas the one in the Animal Kingdom is a live-action multimedia performance.

Whether or not you find its America the Beautiful-and-Perfect boosterism a tad overbearing, not to mention chauvinistic and (despite some rewriting and new narration by Maya Angelou) a bit racist, *The Hall of Presidents* is a mechanical marvel. Honest Abe, veteran of the 1964 World's Fair and patriarch of Audio-Animatronics, rising to his feet is still a moving sight (no pun intended); and the period costuming is, as always with Disney, authentic right down to the hand stitching. But it's fairly slow going, sonorous enough to put some people to sleep while others are getting misty-eyed; although it's a don't-miss for some people, visitors who are planning to see *The American Adventure* in Epcot can wait for that similar but somewhat smoother production. (The unfortunate drawback of having even living presidents on the stage is that you can't help but notice how unlifelike the robots are, because they are so familiar; it actually detracts from the effectiveness of the others. Also, as humanlike as the faces of such Audio-Animatronic figures are, their robotic mouths just aren't as flexible as the real thing, so those with hearing difficulties used to lip-reading will probably want to get either a hearing-assist or reflective captioning device in the lobby.)

We're not as strong as some people about the *Country Bear Jamboree;* admittedly, we're not crazy about those corny, hillbilly hoe-down jokes that even a child can laugh at. The Audio-Animatronic bears are cute, and the music's catchy enough; but with so many other possibilities, we'd use this only as a backup. For similar reasons (cow-patty humor, boot-stompin' and hol-lerin'), we are only lukewarm about *The Diamond Horseshoe Saloon Revue,* but many people, especially country music fans and older visitors who prefer to sit down and watch the show, like both of them quite well. (Both are wheelchair accessible.) Also, you can eat a sandwich while seeing the saloon show, which is convenient. However, if you're the shy sort, don't get too close to the stage; audience members are usually drafted for "dramatic" duty.

Big Thunder Mountain Railroad is a fairly exhilarating roller coaster, based on the idea (a common one among Disney World thrill rides, but well-executed here) that the gold rush train you're riding in has suddenly broken apart and is plunging headlong through the mines and shanty town. It hits speeds of about 28 miles an hour, the same as the more famously terrifying Space Mountain; if lines at the nearby Splash Mountain are too long for you, this is a more than satisfying substitute. The usual neck and back restrictions apply, but mildly; this is more of the old-fashioned slide-to-one-side sort of ride than a big dipper.

The Swiss Family Robinson Treehouse is a personal favorite, partly because of the book and partly because it's the castle of all treehouses, with its multiple stories, clever jerry-rigging, and sheer mechanical wizardry. The drawback for some people will be that it's a walk-through attraction, with stairs and ramps, though no ladders. It's the sort of attraction that requires you to use your own imagination for the action, whereas most others supply you with more external stimuli than you can handle. It's just a matter of taste.

If you like a bit of a thrill and chill, but aren't sure you're up to Space Mountain, you can try Astro Orbiter in Tomorrowland, which will take you back to the days of the traveling State Fairs, or the Mad Tea Party in Fantasyland, which will really remind you of those pack-'em-in carnivals.

Don't Bother

There is a lot here to miss, too: the mini-racing cars on the Tomorrowland Speedway (unless you're a former soap box derby demon), for instance. Most adults can do entirely without Mickey's Toontown Fair unless you want to grab a piece of fruit at the market there or get autographs from the characters; much of Fantasyland, except for the exceptions already mentioned, should be treated as a carnival sideshow.

Though some people will argue, we think you can dispense with the Jungle Cruise, particularly if you are planning to go to Animal Kingdom; though it was a star in its day, it is to newer rides as Saturday morning cartoons are, well, to Disney animation. The creaky old robotic animals are put to shame by generations of later Animatronics, and the "hostile natives" are another anachronistic embarrassment Disney should have gotten rid of.

Similarly, the exotic birds in the Enchanted Tiki Lodge are cute to look at, but after 15 minutes of elementary-school puns, you'll wish you'd waited for the fowl language and real tricks of Flights of Wonder at the Animal Kingdom.

And of course, you know how we feel about It's a Small Whatchamacallit. Don't even go there.

Tips and Tales

As we mentioned, there are several very gentle options in the Magic Kingdom for the less active visitor. Most are what might be called "drive-bys," including the Walt Disney World Railroad, which circles the entire Magic Kingdom and offers a pleasant view of most of the theme areas; the Skyway gondola, which passes from Tomorrowland to a Swiss chalet-like stop in Fantasyland, offering not only a short cut for tired visitors but also a really nice vista; and the Tomorrowland Transit Authority, which is a so-so passage around Tomorrowland laced with annoying ads for Federal Express, but which does include glimpses inside Space Mountain and other attractions. In fact, in the winter months when Space Mountain is being refurbished, you can sometimes see the "skeleton" of the roller coaster exposed to the light. The Liberty Belle Riverboat is a pleasant way to circumnavigate Tom Sawyer Island. Don't forget the horse-drawn wagons that go around Main Street from City Hall; that's a real period piece.

There is live-action street entertainment all the time at the Magic Kingdom (as there is in all the parks), including patriotic proclamations at the Liberty Tree, shoot-'em-ups that erupt in Frontierland, musicians, parades (usually about 3 p.m. and just before closing), musical groups of all flavors, and, of course, the nightly fireworks. You could just wander the streets and be fully entertained.

Here's some Imagineering trivia: Big Thunder Mountain Railroad, at 197 feet tall, is the highest peak in the state of Florida. It was inspired by the mountains of Monument Valley (director John Ford's favorite film setting), took two years to build, and weighs something like 65 tons. Stop for a moment to squint at Space Mountain to see if you recognize it: Despite its high-tech finish, it was formed in the likeness of Japan's lovely Mt. Fuji.

The Swiss Family Robinson Treehouse is 90 feet high, 90 feet wide, and nearly as deep; weighs 200 tons; and has 1,400 branches and more than 300,000 individually attached plastic leaves.

Also, don't leave Main Street without giving the buildings a good hard look, too: They are small masterpieces of optical illusion. The street-level floors are all nearly life-sized, just shrunk to about 90%; but the second stories are at 80%, and the occasional third floors are 60% real size; the diminishing lines appear to make the whole town seem bigger—the buildings taller, the street wider, and the promenade to the Castle longer.

Epcot

Epcot, or at least the Future World half, was supposed to be the real-life Tomorrowland. The acronym originally stood for the Experimental Prototype Community of Tomorrow, and it was to be Walt Disney's great vindication, the proof that science and technology could and would make human life better. Unfortunately, Walt died before his vision of a humane metropolis could be brought to the drawing board; instead, Epcot became a sort of permanent new-technology showcase or super-industry convention. And these days, when the pavilions are "sponsored" by mega-corporations, Walt's faith that science would make the good life both simpler and more affordable seems a little misplaced.

Fortunately, however, there is still the World Showcase, the other half of Epcot, a sort of permanent World's Fair: part 3D travelogue, part museum blockbuster, and part shopping mall/food court. The World Showcase is a vacation in itself, and if you had to pick only one area to visit, it would certainly be a strong contender.

(Frankly, one wonders why Future World and the World Showcase are still joined at the hip: It seems a partnership for which there is little logical explanation, since "culture" and "coexistence" are a far cry from "competition" and "global influence." Not to mention that the World Showcase, with its re-created Eiffel Tower, Mayan temple, Norwegian fjord, and clearly pre-Communist Chinese pavilion, looks back before the twentieth century, much less the twenty-first. It has the unfortunate effect, intentional or not, of suggesting that it is only American technology that will be capable of fulfilling the human destiny—you know, the one to the stars. Let's just hope that by then "multinational" has a more beneficial meaning.)

Recognize right up front that Epcot is big—bigger than the Magic Kingdom and Disney-MGM Studios combined—and time consuming. Also remember that Future World opens earlier and (with a few exceptions) closes earlier than the World Showcase, and plan your time accordingly. Look for the Tip Board, which in this case is right near the entrances.

THE LAYOUT

Epcot is shaped like a great top-heavy hourglass or egg timer, with Future World as the lower half (and the great geodesic sphere of Spaceship Earth as the base weight) and the World Showcase, which is laid out around a huge lagoon, as the upper half. You traverse the two halves by swinging in circles, as in the Magic Kingdom, but even more formalized: Future World is built around a large, round plaza with twin exposition halls and the major pavilions beyond that; and the bridge between Future World and the World Showcase would, if extended in a straight line, run smack into the American Adventure pavilion. (Yep, that's the good ol' U. S. of A.—sitting on top of the world.)

Spaceship Earth sits like a giant silver golf ball on a tee just inside the entrance plaza. Behind that are the two concave wings of Innoventions East and Innoventions West, and they represent the same sort of hub that the garden in front of Cinderella Castle does in the Magic Kingdom; beyond the two plazas are the now-familiar spokes leading to the pavilions. Off to the right (the west) are the Living Seas, The Land, and Imagination Institute; off to the right (east) are the Universe of Energy, Wonders of Life, and what is now Test Track, the newest super-speed thrill ride at Epcot.

The World Showcase can also be divided into two great semicircles, with the American Adventure as the midpoint. As you cross the bridge from Future World toward the lagoon, the pavilions on your right, starting at the bottom and then going up and around counterclockwise, are Canada and the United Kingdom. You cross a little bridge over a canal that leads to the BoardWalk and Beach Club Resort hotel area, then you see France (easily identifiable by the Eiffel Tower), Morocco, the stately Japan, and the American Adventure. If you turned to your left and started around the lagoon, you would first pass Mexico, then Norway, then China, another small bridge to Germany, Italy (whose campanile tower stands as a sort of counterpart to the Eiffel Tower), and back to the American Adventure.

If you want to take a shortcut instead of walking all the way around the lagoon (it's around a mile and a quarter), there are shuttle boats from the foot of the central bridge that head off in a sort of V to either of two docks; one lands at the foot of Morocco, and the other is near Germany. The gondolas at Italy are, alas, only for show. These rides are pleasant on a hot day, because of the breeze, and good for the foot-weary, but they aren't necessarily shortcuts in terms of time, incidentally; if you're a fairly good walker, and you're anxious to get back to the monorail for a dinner reservation or something, you may beat the boat back to the bridge.

Although we have ranked these pavilions, nearly all have something worth at least a glimpse. Fortunately, as mentioned in "Part Eight: Drinking and Dining," you need never hunger or thirst in the World Showcase. There are plenty of benches, many in lovely garden settings, and shade. And we will point out here that Epcot is particularly well supplied with rest rooms: at the entrance (the traditional spot and one that ought always to be the first stop), in most of the pavilions (thought not all), and in the Odyssey Center, which is a sort of low-key building to your left just as you cross the bridge between Future World and the World Showcase.

Don't Miss

If you judge a park by its "rides," then Future World is going to beat the World Showcase all to bits, because there are only a couple of actual rides in the World Showcase, and neither is very exciting. (One's a complete dud, in fact.) The problem is that Future World is supposed to be a series of educational, high-tech, and intellectually gripping exhibits—and the most successful things, by and large, are the thrill rides. Those intellectual properties are so clearly commercialized that one sometimes feels like a sucker, just they way you do when you buy gasoline from the most convenient station even though the company charges 20 cents a gallon more than anyone else. (This feeling is especially strong when you hear Ellen DeGeneres, on behalf of Exxon, official petroleum company of Walt Disney World and sponsor of the Wonders of Energy pavilion, top off her supposed energy-conservation adventure by reassuring us that there is plenty of fossil fuel left to burn.)

But of course, it's only a problem if you long more for education than stimulation. Having made that point, we can say without reservation that there are some first-class attractions at Future World, starting with *Honey, I Shrunk the Audience,* one of several brilliant 3D attractions around Walt Disney World. *Honey,* in the Imagination Institute pavilion, is a take-off from the popular Rick Moranis (Disney studios) movie, *Honey, I Shrunk the Kids,* and the setup film stars Moranis in his original absent-minded professor role. But in this version, the shrinking ray is inadvertently turned on the audience members, who are then bombarded with scents, visual effects, laser beams, tactile effects (no, we won't ruin it for you), and played-for-laugh scares. It lasts about 17 minutes; though there is usually a line, there is some entertainment provided in the queue. This is a sit-down attraction, but requires wearing special glasses, so those with visual problems may not get the full effect. And if you're in a wheelchair, it won't be quite the same, either (but almost).

Body Wars is a sort of intestinal twin to the extraterrestrial Star Tours ride in the Disney-MGM Studios park, only with a script lifted from *Fantastic Voyage.* Instead of being trapped in a space transport reeling out of control at light speed, passengers in Body Wars are in research pods that have been shrunk (again) to the size of a blood cell and injected into a human body. This ride uses flight simulators to imitate the pulsation of the blood stream, the careening speed of the circulation, and so on. But though this is only a mild problem for the neck, it can be a serious threat to the stomach—major motion-sickness territory. If you can make it through the aorta without gasping, you've a stronger stomach than mine, Gunga Din. An unfortunate number of people who boast of being nausea-proof have regretted it here (and so have their neighbors). However, this ride also depends on brilliantly executed film to fool your mind, and hence your body, into such dizziness, so if you shut your eyes, you'll be fine.

Test Track is sponsored by General Motors, which makes a vague gesture toward encouraging safe driving habits with this simulated race-track roller coaster ride, but if you believe that argument, there's an opening for a new crash-test dummy. It can't be denied that as thrill rides go, this one, which is rumored to push the 65 mph speed limit (although officials say only 45), is a doozy. The track includes hairpin turns, dips and climbs, and quite scary side-to-side swaying, plus a pretty architectural pun that has the track busting through a wall of the building into the open air. The "cars" are based on the same flight simulator units as Body Wars and Star Tours, and, oh, did we mention that these sporty little convertibles have neither steering wheels nor brakes? Test Track is notoriously undependable about hours—it has been opened, closed, renovated, tuned up, opened, debugged, retested, and reopened several times, but as time goes on, it's settling in. Needless to say, Sunday drivers and back-seat ones need not apply.

The other best bet in Future World—and the only serious attraction—is The Living Seas. It's only partly a ride (a simulated descent into an underwater research station), and mostly an exhibit, but in fact much of the marine experimentation going on is real: The pavilion houses a 27-foot-tall tank that reproduces the ocean ecosphere, and there are an unusual number of interactive exhibits that suggest what Future World might have been. If you don't have time to stop, but you love aquariums, consider having dinner in the Coral Reef Restaurant: The whole front "wall" is an eight-inch glass window onto the tank, and each table has full-color identification guides to the rainbow of passing fish. (And no, you're not eating those guys.)

The World Showcase is a whole other kettle of fish. In fact, it's a whole other rainbow—the human sort. Instead of being rather passively carried along in the arms of (either real or simulated) technology, as in Future World, visitors to the World Showcase have the opportunity to step into another culture and another time; to speak with live, not programmed, cast members from the various countries; and, of course, to bring back "souvenirs" of other countries as if you had actually visited them. (It might be worth looking through "Part Ten: Shopping in Walt Disney World" before choosing your route.) The World Showcase may not be so high-tech as Future World, but oddly enough, it does seem more genuinely educational—a form of Disney diplomacy.

As we said, you should at least stroll around all the pavilions of the World Showcase, but if your time or stamina is limited, there are some that really stand out: France, Morocco, Japan (which, as suggested in the shopping chapter, are the three neighboring countries, at least in this World, that even if you only have an hour you must make time for), and China.

Japan's complex is classically lovely, with its five-story pagoda, copied from a seventh-century temple in Nara, an early capitol; its carefully executed but intentionally "natural" gardens and waterfall; and the long restaurant/shopping wing modeled on the Imperial Palace in Kyoto. There is no formal show or ride here, but a variety of live performers—mimes, puppeteers, storytellers, and troupes of kodo drum musicians, who have to be as much athletes as drummers, of the sort that have been touring the United States for the last few years—appear in the courtyard. There are several kinds of food available here, from quick-grilled chicken (yakitori) to table-top teppanyaki and even a lovely, though limited, sushi bar; all of the food here is good. You might be surprised how long you find you've lingered here. (We hesitate to mention it, but this is a great place to view the *Illumi-Nations* show.)

Morocco doesn't have a formal stage, either, but it has a lively tumbling troupe that barrels around the plaza (their performance times are listed on a small board) and a belly dancer who entertains in the Marrakesh restaurant at night (where the food is also very good). The small art museum is fine, and even if you don't intend to buy anything, wander through the mini-casbah long enough to admire the authentic tilework, the hand-knotted rugs, and to savor the incense of the place.

It's hard to imagine that anyone isn't predisposed to love the French pavilion, with its turn-of-the-century benches, perfumes and pastries, alleys and, especially, glasses of wine in the shade. The food in the French pavilion is—as in Japan and Morocco— some of the best in Epcot, and the view from the sidewalk tables, though not perhaps as astonishing as the real Parisian view, is fairly amazing. France has one of the three travelogue films in the World Showcase—the most evocative one, if you only want to see a single example. (Though these movies are all nice, they tend to follow a sort of format that becomes a little obvious and repetitious if you see them too close together.) Mimes, balloon-twisters, and occasional living mannequins sometimes appear in the place.

The China pavilion is a true must-see, both inside and out. Along with one of the two Circle-Vision 360 films, it has lovely exhibits on indigenous peoples of that huge nation, a half-size reproduction of the Temple of Heaven in Beijing, and the most beautiful gardens of this garden-rich park, an entire complex of tea houses, benches, lotus ponds, and meditation paths. Plan to linger here, too. Don't plan to eat.

The last best-best in the World Showcase has to be qualified, because it's not always best and not always even open. The American Gardens Theater, a pleasant amphitheater on the lagoon across from the U.S. pavilion, showcases international dance troupes, acrobatic companies, choruses, musical groups, and comedians who book engagements of several weeks. Some of these are very good indeed, although whether you're interested in a particular show may depend on how tired you are and what else you have scheduled. Showtimes (all free, of course) are listed on a board outside the exits.

Second Best

In this case, the "seconds" could be called the "best of the rest," because most all of it is pretty entertaining. Spaceship Earth, although it may suggest Space Mountain, is a very gentle and pleasant ride through human history and into the presumed future, with the emphasis on the development of communication: first speech, then writing, then the press, mass media, computers, the Internet, and so on. (As it frequently reminds you, it's sponsored by AT&T.) Riders pass Audio-Animatronic mini-dramas and dioramas ranging from prehistoric cave drawings to ancient Greece, Leonardo Da Vinci's studio, a 1950s family rec room (with Walt Disney himself on the TV), futuristic cities under the ocean and others on far planets all hooked together by an interstellar form of the Web. It does have nice mechanical effects and a fine uplifting climax that is supposed to bring a sentimental mist to your eyes, but don't be surprised if you find it just a trifle . . . smug. No jolts, terrors, or difficulty with this one. Riders with hearing difficulties may find that the sound effects of various scenes sometimes overlap one another, an unavoidable consequence of having continual-feed trains going by; but it's not a major problem.

Whether or not you're headed for Body Wars, you should consider *Cranium Command,* also in the Wonders of Life pavilion, which is a 20-minute animated show about, well, a pubescent boy's brain. (Be sure to see the introductory cartoon, explaining who the Brain Pilots-in-training are, or it won't make much sense.) It's the sort of thing only a parent or Woody Allen fan could truly love; but even childless couples who survived high school will probably have some fun with it.

If you're not brave or balanced enough for Test Track, you can still go into the Test Track Exhibits area and play around with various forms of dashboard technology, on-board navigational systems, and so on. And guess what? There's lots of GM merchandise and even some shiny new cars to look at.

Among the optional destinations at the World Showcase (starting from the right of the bridge again): Canada is visually stunning and a clever expression of the nation's cultural diversity, with its great Anglo-Canadian stone mansion, French-Canadian streetscape, and Native American totem poles. Its Circle-Vision 360 film is shown in an underground "cavern" that is a really pleasant retreat in hot weather; the steakhouse is underground, too, though that may be one of its better features. The walkway may be a little steep for some.

The United Kingdom complex is a small group of shops with facades that run the gamut from country cottage to London swank. Whether or not you go through them, you should definitely stop for a moment to enjoy not only the rose garden in front but also the little formal garden in the back; Eeyore, among other characters, is known to nuzzle around back there. On the other side of the road, that is, on the lagoon side, is the Rose and Crown pub, which is a highlight, and for those with publican leanings, might even be a best bet. The outdoor tables are obviously front-row seats for *IllumiNations,* although equally obviously, other people have already noticed that, so make your move early. Note that this is a bar and smoking is allowed inside, a fact that seems to be on the smokers' grapevine.

There isn't much to the United States pavilion other than *The American Adventure,* the Audio-Animatronic show there; and if you've already been to *The Hall of Presidents,* you can probably pass on this. Of course, if you were moved to patriotic tears at that production, you'll want to get right in line. But be warned: If you're a woman, minority, or open-minded male majority member, you may find yourself a little embarrassed, because if Spaceship Earth offers an idealized version of human evolution, *The American Adventure* offers an even more clean-and-shiny version of human (and industrial) revolution. It reminds you of a contest: Tell us everything you love about America in 30 minutes or less. Also, the pavilion is something of a design embarrassment: With all the dramatic and detailed architecture visible around the World Showcase, the U.S. pavilion looks like the "deluxe" two-story model in a suburban cluster development. (Well, we did warn you that this was going to be the opinionated chapter.)

Germany is boisterous, bouncy, sausage-fragrant, and relentlessly musical: In other words, you'll either love it or hate it. Cast members (and not infrequently, visitors) yodel and polka, which of course means the tuba oompers are playing while you bite the bratwurst. Do make sure to stop by the model railroad layout just to the right (toward Italy); Walt Disney was a lifelong railroad enthusiast—he even worked very briefly as a porter when young—which is why there are so many trains around the parks.

Italy, like many of the pavilions consigned to "second-best" class here, is charming to walk through, and that's really all you need to do. If you have a few minutes to spare or need to rest a while, its mini-piazza, with its tall pines and Venetian bell tower, is a lovely spot.

The major thrill ride of the World Showcase, such as it is, is Norway's Maelstrom, a fairly fun but brief combination white-water river ride and hail-the-Vikings, duck-the-trolls fantasy. But it comes attached to a film promoting Norwegian tourism, which is somewhat annoying (though the countryside is certainly attractive). The rest of the complex is really pretty, especially the wooden stave church, and if you're into smoked meats and cheeses, the buffet, in the replica fourteenth-century Akershus, is definitely hearty.

Don't Bother

To be fair, Ellen's Energy Adventure could go into the "Second Best" category, except that it is so overhyped and annoying. It wants to be very hip (MTV-style multiple screens, anomie humor, gay-cult comedienne Ellen DeGeneres), but it's so predictable (unless you slept through third grade) and so static that it's a real disappointment. The setup, and the vast majority of the ride itself, involves a two-layer dream-sequence sitcom: Level one, Ellen DeGeneres gets on an energy quiz show with a high school rival and, when she starts to lose, leaps into one of those time-warp second-level sitcoms with Bill Nye, the Science Guy, and finds herself back in Jurassic Parkland. The one "active" segment of the ride, along a river with dinosaurs, is fun, but the animals are sort of mid-generation—better than the ones in Spaceship Earth, but not as good as in Countdown to Extinction at Animal Kingdom—so they start to seem repetitive.

Similarly, Innoventions West has many fans, but it's the sort of high-tech playground that will delight computer-game vets, intrigue some Internet novices, and absolutely terrify (and possibly deafen) many others. Although it's supposed to be a showcase for online and satellite technologies, it's more like a huge Sega arcade (yes, with brand names), with advance teasers for next season's merchandise (virtual reality games, new gadgets). The best thing for most older adults will be to get into the free Internet postcard booth, send a message to your family saying you're surviving, check your email if you have any, and keep moving. After all, even if you are an online-game fan, why spend money and time playing at Disney World when you can do it at home? Although designed to be wheelchair-accessible, it's usually crowded, confusingly laid out, weirdly lit because of all the machines, and janglingly loud. Innoventions East is scarcely distinguishable from a souvenir shop.

The Land is pleasant enough, and the Living with the Land ride through the hydroponic gardens is relaxing, but there is more video than real experience and very little in the way of new information, unless you're still having trouble spelling the word *environment.* Besides, all of the plants except those in the greenhouses —where teaching underdeveloped nations to grow plants sounds a lot more like market development than one-world preservation —are artificial. You'd do better to take the Behind the Seeds tour of the greenhouses (see "Part Seven: Adult Education"). If you do go in, you might get an easy smile out of the Audio-Animatronic veggies of *Food Rocks*—Chubby Cheddar, Neil Moussaka, Pita Gabriel, and so on singing things like "Tutti-Frutti"—but don't schedule your day around it.

Unless you still need help with sex education—or you're pregnant and sentimental—skip *The Making of Me,* which does Disney credit for its frank and funny treatment of the birds and the bees, but is aimed at kids. Of course, they already know all about it . . .

Although the Maelstrom is some fun, the El Río del Tiempo boat ride inside the Mexico pavilion is not. In fact, although it only lasts about seven minutes, "the river of time" seems endless. Except for the music, which is only slightly more sophisticated than It's a Small World, and the somewhat more violent suggestion of Aztec human sacrifice, you could be back in the dollhouse. The only interesting feature of the entire circuit is the "smoking" volcano, and you can see that from the entire pavilion.

Tips and Tales

Some of the most fun at Epcot is right in front of your eyes. Or under your feet. Like the "Mom, I Can't Believe It's Disney!" fountain on the walkway near Journey into Imagination, which erupts at musical and sprightly random intervals from the concrete. You can easily duck it, if you want, but it's so charming—and you don't get all that wet (unless you want to). There's a somewhat more choreographed water ballet every 15 minutes from the fountain in the middle of the Innoventions Plaza straight behind Spaceship Earth, a "dancing water" show (really nicest after dark, when colored lights are added), and a sort of World Showcase Lagoon in miniature, since two dozen countries around the world collected water from home to be combined for this fountain.

Other fun facts: Spaceship Earth is 180 feet tall, the same as Space Mountain; it may be the only permanent geospheric structure in the world, going Buckminster Fuller's famous geodesic dome one better.

As mentioned above, all the plants in the Living with the Land ride, except for those in the greenhouses, are artificial. But then, so is the ocean water in the Coral Reef. And so is the reef.

Disney-MGM Studios

Call it self-absorption, call it self-promotion, call it chutzpah, but whatever you call it, Disney-MGM Studios is a masterpiece of integrated marketing. The parades re-create some Disney features (most recently *Mulan* and *Aladdin*), the live-action shows play on others (*Hunchback of Notre Dame, The Little Mermaid,* and *Beauty and the Beast*), the production stages promote at least one recent Disney release (Backstage Pass to . . .), and one upcoming feature (*The Making of* . . .). The nightly light/dancing waters/fireworks/laser spectacular, *Fantasmic!,* manages to recycle the characters from a dozen different Disney films, tying them loosely together with a lot of *Fantasia* imagery just in time to build interest in the release of *Fantasia 2000.* The only outside movie figures who make much of an appearance are cult heroes who are safely deceased (Rod Serling and Jim Henson, whose partnership with Disney was not exactly amicable) or who have made no secret of their admiration for Disney, such as George Lucas and Steven Spielberg. (For more on this subject, see "Part Nine: 'Hidden Mickeys' and Other Grown-Up Games.")

In other words, Disney-MGM Studios is one huge greatest-hits collection—not unlike a live version of what MGM itself did in the *That's Entertainment* movies. This may be a theme park that nominally salutes the craft of great movie-making in general, but its underlying theme, suggested by the ordering of "Disney" and "MGM" in the title, is that Disney alone still has the spirit of the good ol' Tinseltown days. It's almost Lincolnesque in a perverse way: a park dedicated to the proposition that this great commercial enterprise, of the Disney people, by the Disney people, for the Disney people (the audience, presumably), shall not vanish from your thoughts for a moment. In fact, pretty soon they may have to start calling it Disney-MGM-ABC Studios, to explain those other minor promotional appearances by ABC soap opera stars and other network symbols.

THE LAYOUT

Although the layout of Disney-MGM is not quite as easily grasped as that of the other three parks—there aren't actual bridges or defined mini-parks, just paths and clusters of buildings—there is some remnant of the tree pattern to it. Fortunately, this is the smallest of the parks, so even if you go the long way around, you'll eventually find everything.

This time the trunk of the tree is an art deco era Hollywood Boulevard. A big, low branch, Sunset Boulevard shoots off to the right about halfway up the trunk. At the end of this branch you'll find the Twilight Zone Tower of Terror, the Rock 'n' Roller Coaster, and the entrance to *Fantasmic!* Continuing up the trunk, you arrive at what passes for a central hub—a parade circle around a little garden pool.

On the far side of the circle at the top of the trunk is The Great Movie Ride. To the right is the Studio Arch—which one can only see as Disney's official Arc de Triomphe. Passing through the Arch, the animation tour is ahead and to the right, and the *Voyage of the Little Mermaid* is to the left on Mickey Avenue. If you continue down Mickey Avenue, you'll encounter the Studios Backlot Tour and Backstage Pass, a tour through the working Studios soundstages.

Back at the hub, a left turn will take you to the Echo Lake section of the park, with the *Indiana Jones Epic Stunt Spectacular*, Disney's Doug Live!, the *ABC Sound Studio*, and Star Tours. If you turn right at Star Tours you'll enter the New York Street Back Lot set and Muppet Plaza. Attractions in this area include a Muppets 3-D movie, a stageshow musical rendition of the *Hunchback of Notre Dame,* and a kids' play area.

Don't Miss

The park's two big draws, the Tower of Terror and the Rock 'n' Roller Coaster, sit side by side at the end of Sunset Boulevard.

The Twilight Zone Tower of Terror has a new twist guaranteed to line 'em up: not one, not two, but three seriously terrifying drops that will leave your stomach in a tumult. The story is set up like an old *Twilight Zone* episode, complete with Rod Serling intro (notice that his ever-present cigarette has been "lifted" from the video) and lots of TV series trivia; in this case, the luxury hotel you're supposedly staying in is caught in a time warp where its disastrous last night goes on forever a la *The Shining.* With that series of shocks, sort of like the slasher monster who keeps reappearing after he's supposedly dead, it packs a helluva wallop. This ride is not, obviously, for those with weak vertebrae or stomachs; but the setting itself is so elaborate and detailed that visitors who aren't going to actually take the elevator itself can stay in line up to that point, then ask the attendant for the safer shortcut out. Blackout alert, too.

The Rock 'n' Roller Coaster is Disney's answer to the Universal Islands of Adventure thrill-ride challenge. Instead of clanking to the top of a hill and then letting gravity do the rest, the Rock 'n' Roller hurls you up the hill (at 60 mph, no less) and flings you into a series of loops, dips, twists, and turns that may have you hurling by the time the thing stops. All of this, of course, in the dark with rock music blasting in your ears. Our advice is to take this ride seriously: Space Mountain is Bambi compared to the

Rock 'n' Roller Coaster. Both the Rock 'n' Roller Coaster and the Tower of Terror stay jammed all day, so try to ride both during the first half hour the park is open.

Star Tours is the third most popular attraction in this park and, with the release of *The Phantom Menace*, will be getting another attendance boost, so either get there early, go at nap time, or expect to stand in line. Scratch it right off the list, however, if you get dizzy, motion-sick, disoriented, or have moderate to severe neck trouble; this is a major thrill chill. Like Body Wars and Countdown to Extinction, it uses a NASA flight simulator chassis as "cars," and once the flight is out of control (you knew that it would be, of course; there are only a few great plots in thrill rides), the bucking, pitching, yawing, and exacerbating visual effects really take over. It's not quite as nauseating as Body Wars, as least in our experience, but it's certainly challenging. Claustrophobics need not apply, either.

Moving on to other more tame amusements, the Great Movie Ride really is like a version of *That's Entertainment,* only with Audio-Animatronic figures mixed in with the re-created sets and film clips. Waiting in line for this ride is no problem, except for standing around some more, because the overhead monitors have loops of great movie scenes and faces, like those Academy Award highlight montages. Some of the scenes are just re-creations, like the one from *Raiders of the Lost Ark* (which, after all, is reenacted just over the way at the *Indiana Jones Epic Stunt Spectacular*); some have music and action (the pop-up Munchkins of *The Wizard of Oz,* the fly-up Mary Poppins), and some are just famous snippets ("Top o' the world, Ma!"). There's even a bit of *Singin' in the Rain* that you yourself can reenact (if you can dance, that is) on the New York Street Backlot, where an umbrella hangs on a "raining" light pole in Gene Kelly's honor. This ride is a universal hit: no jolts, shocks, or blackouts, though the overlapping soundtracks of the scenes, as in most of the sequential rides, can be muddled for those with hearing difficulties.

The New York Street Backlot, incidentally, used to be visible only if you took the larger Backlot Tour, and then you went through on a tram; nowadays, it's a little attraction in itself, with a bookstore, lovely lampposts, and amazing period details (Hollywood perfect, of course). Throughout the Thanksgiving to

New Year's period, the New York Street is the center of the massive lights display described in Part One.

The Magic of Disney Animation should be on everybody's list: There is no "ride" to it, so no discomfort warnings; no special effects except for the very real art of the animators (and some dizzying blather from the ubiquitous Robin Williams). To some extent you can pace your own tour; it starts with one film and ends with another, but in between, if you're happy to sit quietly and watch through the windows, you can spend as much time as you like watching the artists at work. You see how gels, cels, and backdrops are created and put together—occasionally you can see artists working on an actual upcoming feature, though not always—and one of the highlights is a greatest hits montage from Disney animation film. (Okay, so it's more self-promotion, but this is the field they earned it in.)

Jim Henson's MuppetVision 4D is one of those things that sounds childish (and in many ways is), but few people are immune to the various charms of the Muppets, and in any case, the effects are spectacular. Whether it was just the luck of seating on our last visit, the 3D effects of this show seemed even more powerful than those at *It's Tough to Be a Bug* or *Honey, I Shrunk the Audience.* Cool, sweet, and undemanding.

Second Best

The Studio Backlot Tour used to be a must-see, back when it included what is now the New York Street Backlot and Backstage Pass segments. Most people will still enjoy it; but it's dropped to the alternative list because now it comes across more as just another collection of special effects how-to's (though the Catastrophe Canyon set is sort of fun), wardrobes and costumes, miniatures, props and construction, animation, and so on. Some of it is very interesting, some of it verges on the cutesy, and if you do all the various "industry" tours in the park, a lot of it is redundant. But it's a nonthreatening excursion—a little walking but mostly tram riding, and good for all ages.

Many people still love the *Indiana Jones Epic Stunt Spectacular,* and it does have its moments; but stunt work isn't nearly as much of a mystery or a secret as it used to be. After all, we have had commercials, TV series, and movies all starring stunt men. The other thing is that the Spielberg films themselves are so incredibly well made that these copies don't seem nearly so impressive. Depending on the cast members that particular day, the performance can seem pretty rote, too. But Indy fans and older, less TV-savvy visitors will find this semi-behind-the-scenes view fascinating. (Just remember, the "exposed" stuff is fake, too: The sound men, prop men, and director are part of the cast, not the "real" crew.) The spectacle requires a little audience participation, but if you want to be a major part of the action, better be prepared to make a spectacle of yourself.

You will certainly be drawn to see *Fantasmic!*—after all, there's almost nothing else to do at that hour—but if you go, arrive an hour early if you want to score a seat. If you have a choice, try to sit somewhere more or less in the central areas; despite the size of the amphitheater and reassurances that you can see the show from anywhere, it is a lot less impressive from the sides. (If the lights and projections get there ahead of the "mist" that serves as the projection curtain, for instance, it's really a let-down.)

If you want to see one of the three live shows based on animated movies, *Voyage of the Little Mermaid,* which has at least some novelty of plot, is the most attractive and has the catchiest music.

Many people go into the *Beauty and the Beast Stage Show*; most sit through it, and some like it. A number of people who don't have kids to keep them there leave early, however, and it's easy to see why. Sure, the Broadway version is a big hit. Even the ice version is good. But this is elementary school stuff. Rent the video.

Both *Beauty and the Beast* and *The Hunchback of Notre Dame* serve up Disney animated features as live musical production shows. *Beauty* is pretty straightforward (been there—done that), but *Hunchback* breaks some new ground with its presentation and staging.

The Backstage Pass Tour focuses on a Disney film. If you liked the flick, you might want to see the stuff (a lot of people go into the *101 Dalmatians* tour just to see Cruella's car). This is a walk-through, though, not a sit-down.

Don't Bother

Disney's Doug Live! may amuse some children, but most adults will find it vacuous, if not downright painful.

ABC Sound Studio "exposes" sound-effects secrets through a little story starring Drew Carey.

We wouldn't even bother to tell you to avoid the *Honey I Shrunk the Kids* movie set playground if it weren't placed so confusingly that many visitors find themselves wandering into it looking for the Studio Backlot Tour. Keep your eyes open.

Tips and Tales

Despite the fact that its apparent "spire" is the blasted roof of The Twilight Zone Tower of Terror, Disney-MGM does have a sort of castle at its heart, too: the replica of Mann's Chinese Theater, for many years known as Graumann's Chinese, an ornate and luxurious cinema from Hollywood's heyday.

Mann's rather thoughtfully mirrors the positioning of Cinderella Castle in the Magic Kingdom. Cinderella Castle may be, architecturally, simply the more elaborate successor to the older Sleeping Beauty's Castle at California's Disneyland. But by the time Disney World was being designed, almost 20 years after Disneyland, Walt Disney and his merry band of Imagineers were far more experienced, maybe a little less naive, and a lot more fiscally sophisticated. The popularity of *Cinderella* had rescued the dangerously strapped Disney Studios from certain financial collapse, and so it was not only the symbol of animated movie-making at its finest but also at its most commercially successful. Cinderella herself had become a sort of movie idol. And the Magic Kingdom was a park that re-created Disney's own film and TV productions—the animated features in Fantasyland, the live-action movies in Adventureland and Frontierland.

So when it came time to choose a centerpiece for Disney-MGM Studios, a park that saluted the movie-making industry in a much broader fashion (but which promoted Disney's productions just as fervently), the Imagineers settled on a replica of Mann's Chinese Theater, which was the symbol of Hollywood filmmaking at its best and most successful. It was where Hollywood's most glittering premieres were staged, and where stars and celebrities who had "made it" were invited to put their handprints and autographs in the cement of the sidewalk. The Imagineers re-created the theater, and they re-created the handprints. Then they put the print of Cinderella's tiny glass slipper there, too.

Disney's Animal Kingdom

It may seem a little odd that in a kingdom built around a talking mouse, it took so long to built this castle for creatures. But perhaps it was because Mickey was so very human that he seemed to be more on our side of the animal divide. After all, even in Disney cartoons, there are more and less real creatures: Goofy is a cartoon, but Pluto is at least half-real, and all the various breeds in *101 Dalmatians* are real. Robin Hood is a purely fantastical fox, whereas the eponymous kit of the *Fox and the Hound* is real. Alice's White Rabbit is a cartoon, but Bambi's friend Thumper was real. Even the dragon in *Pete and the Dragon* is a cartoon, though the queenly creature in *Sleeping Beauty* is shiveringly real.

And then, there's the question of budgets and support staff. Celluloid mice only eat celluloid cheese, and that's easy and cheap to come by and has no digestive by-products, either. Taking responsibility for the permanent care of hundreds of thousands of animals in addition to those already populating the park—and in a time of Hollywood-led pro-animal activism—must have been daunting indeed.

Nevertheless, however long it took to create this park, and whatever the costs involved (an estimated $1 billion), it is a stunning success. It's huge—more than 500 acres, five times the size of the Magic Kingdom—and is almost strikingly restrained in the sort of commercial tie-ins that fill the other parks. Aside from Camp Minnie-Mickey, you are likely to see only some rather infectious insect toys inspired by *It's a Bug's Life* and the inevitable safari-suited Barbie and Mickey. In general, it's the animals who are the stars of this kingdom.

Among the species are okapi, nyala, Thompson's gazelles, sable antelope, white-bearded wildebeest, bongoes, scimitar-horned oryx, elands, and Mhorr gazelles; guinea fowl, flamingos, yellow-billed storks, Marabou storks, Egyptian geese, and Abyssinian ground hornbills; cheetahs, lions, and tigers; hippopotamuses and black and white rhinos; Mandrills, silverbacks, and baboons; ostriches; zebras and elephants. Not to mention that old *Carnotaurus*.

Disney's Animal Kingdom does seem to have made up for its laggardly execution in one way—by building in a Hidden Mickey map profile. Although the territory isn't perfectly reproduced on the park-attraction maps, we seem to see, squinting at the greenery that represents the perimeter plantings, a large round area that starts at the entrance plaza and includes DinoLand U.S.A., Safari Village, Harambe Square, and the Maharaja Jungle Trek area. To the left, Camp Minnie-Mickey sort of sticks out like a little round nose; at the upper left, the green spaces seem to curve high around the Kilimanjaro Safaris savanna and the Conservation Station area, and another bit curves out beyond the Kali River Rapids. Yes, it may be wishful thinking, a false sighting, or even a temporary effect that will be obscured, as at other parks, by future expansion. But we like to think that the spirit of that sweet-tempered mouse, who made all these other creatures, real and imaginary, possible, underlies this fourth-generation park.

Having said that, we should probably address the question of animal injuries and deaths under Disney's care, and the broader issue of caging up wild animals in artificial habitats. We are entirely sympathetic to such concerns and as adamant as any animal rights organization that the quality of care and authenticity of environment be rigorously maintained. We agree that the death of a wild animal while in human custody is a grave failure of responsibility.

However, it is increasingly clear that wildlife conservation is an even graver responsibility. No animal population in any institution can be made injury-proof or invulnerable to illness, but then, neither can any wild animal population. It is quite likely that protected herds are less susceptible to disease, in fact, as well as being free from predators. Unfortunately, the most dangerous predators wild animals face are not other creatures, with whom they could live in a natural balance, but humans, who are poaching and exploiting some species and driving others out of their homes and feeding territories. With the rapid and terrible destruction of their natural habitats, more and more wild animal species are becoming crucially endangered or inbred; without modern zoological parks and preserves, especially those as elaborately researched, constructed, and staffed as the Animal Kingdom, they may vanish altogether. We can only hope that the experiments and conservation studies undertaken here will help us develop even better facilities before that happens.

THE LAYOUT

The touring map of the Animal Kingdom follows the now-familiar tree pattern: a main path from the entrance plaza to a central hub and multiple branches off to self-contained theme areas. Only in this case, the hub itself, and the main symbol of the park, is also a tree, the Tree of Life. While Spaceship Earth pays tribute to the evolution of humanity, the Tree of Life salutes the family of humanity, the animal family. (And, with its mind-boggling optical illusion of a mural, it suggest the evolution of the animal kingdom as well.) So just as the Magic Kingdom's Cinderella Castle and Disney-MGM's Mann's Chinese Theater have a sort of symmetry, so do Epcot's Earth and the Animal Kingdom's Tree.

As you cross the bridge from the entrance area toward the island where the Tree of Life stands, the passage to DinoLand U.S.A. is off to your right and lower down, around 4 o'clock; the bridge to Asia is at about 1:30; to Africa at 10:30 or 11 o'clock; and to Camp Minnie-Mickey at 7 o'clock.

There's another difference: In the other three parks, the way into the main park from the entrance plaza is a fairly straight shot intended to get you right into the action (stopping for film and a souvenir or two, of course). In the Animal Kingdom, however, the pathway itself is an attraction. Not only have the walking surfaces been transformed into "fossil trails" of cobblestones or mud-plastered bricks, but the meandering Oasis, which is the area between the entrance plaza and the bridge to the Tree of Life, is a zoological and botanical garden in its own right, with each little garden plot beautifully landscaped and inhabited by unusual birds, small mammals, and insects with labels to help you identify them. (And sometimes to spot them, as they can be sleeping or shy.) The sidewalk weaves about rather than going straight in; you can choose your own route, sloping down to see the otter environment through its underwater "window" or winding under rock bridges or just following the cries of the toucans and parrots.

Don't Miss

There are two major thrill rides in the Animal Kingdom: Countdown to Extinction in DinoLand U.S.A. and the Kali River Rapids whitewater adventure in the Asia section; plus the Kilimanjaro Safaris, which is less physically exciting (or less physically taxing, depending on your outlook), but has other rewards in terms of wildlife.

Countdown to Extinction is the latest in the Body Wars/Star Tours type simulator adventure, in which captive audiences are suddenly at the mercy of forces—namely, speed and danger—beyond their control. The story in this case is that a company has developed a method of time travel that allows the curious to go back 65 million years to see the dinosaurs at a presumably safe distance; of course, something goes wrong and the hapless humans find themselves trying to outrun a murderous *Carnotaurus* (Disney World veterans will recognize the general storyline.) The time-warp jump isn't much of a jolt, and the actual bumps and jerks and sudden-scary-moment turns are only moderately uncomfortable, but the Audio-Animatronic creatures, especially the you-know-what, are fascinatingly constructed and far more sophisticated than the ones in older attractions around the park. In fact, it's a great thumbnail lesson in how fast such theatrical effects have progressed. (If you want to go along, but have any doubts about the shaking up, ask to be seated in the center of the car rather than at either side or in the front row.)

The Kali River Rapids ride is sort of the 1999 version of the Jungle Cruise, only the threats and upsets of this version, like the dinosaurs of Countdown to Extinction, are far more realistic and detailed. Each "raft" holds about a dozen passengers who are supposedly cruising through an environmentally protected region of the Chakranadi River, but who are warned that illegal logging operations are continuing. The scenery is absolutely stunning, and, as always, meticulously authentic: a classic Indian temple, a Southeast Asian pavilion, and a bamboo grove (where those oversized atomizers that make the Magic Kingdom smell of chocolate cookies here release clouds of jasmine and then, in warning, a burst of woodsmoke). The rafts emerge into a clear-cut field where the bamboo is burning, apparently out of control, matted trees have become hazards in the current, the once-serene river is suddenly swirling . . . And the most intriguing thing about this, since the "script" is more for atmosphere than anything else, is the fact that these rafts are not on preset tracks, but actually respond to the currents and eddies. Don't wear your best or gauziest blouse for this one, as you're undoubtedly going to get wet.

Actually, in terms of script (except for the water), the Kilimanjaro Safaris ride could also be described as the sequel to Jungle Cruise, because it has the pilot-guide with his little microphone, his corny jokes, the supposed warning radioed in from afar, and the not-infrequent glimpses of other jeeps obviously receiving the same story, and so on. Still, it's the hottest ticket at the Animal Kingdom and should be experienced as soon as the park opens, or alternatively, after 5 p.m.

The Kilimanjaro Safaris was one of the most widely publicized attractions in the months prior to Animal Kingdom's opening, and it deservedly draws huge crowds, so be prepared. The "story" is that while taking you on this nice photo safari, the guide stumbles on an elephant-poaching operation and winds up chasing the bad guys. . . . Well, you know the usual plot from here.

But don't let the corniness put you off. This is a major zoo tour on wheels, featuring lions, flamingos, elephants, hippos, and many others, though it's a bit hard to say what animals you will actually see because they all have different eating, sleeping, and social habits. You can take real photographs of the animals, though you can't use a flash and have to be prepared to snap as you drive past (for this reason, paradoxically, an inexpensive autofocus camera is probably better than a fancy 35 mm SLR). The 110-acre savanna was painstakingly re-created, and not the way some other landscapes have been, the ones that were only theatrical sets: Because the animals and birds here actually eat the "backdrop," the shrubs and grasses have to be real (although the trunks of some trees are concrete hung with edible leaves).

Disney staffers turn the animals' erratic schedule into a virtue by suggesting that you could take the ride several times and see different creatures. And it's true; no tour is exactly the same. But you have to listen to the sappy spiel over and over again, which seems utterly expendable and perhaps will vanish eventually. If you can only go once or twice, plan to go in the cool of the morning or evening; the greatest number of the animals will be napping or feeling antisocial at midday, and if you have spent an hour or more in line, and still only see four or five animals, you may be unhappy.

These adventure rides tend to get most of the press and attract the longer lines. The Pagnani Forest Exploration Trail, on the other hand, doesn't get nearly as much attention as the Kilimanjaro Safaris—in fact, just judging by its name, a huge number of people think it's a plain old nature trail and skip it entirely—but it's the real sleeper hit here, a gentle, nearly up-close-and-personal encounter with the animals that is much more moving and satisfying than the theatrical version. This is an absolute must-see; and actually, it the sort of attraction that, although packed with children, is no less enjoyable for that reason because most of the kids are instinctively awed and respectful; their astonishment in this case may increase your own pleasure.

Pagnani is Swahili for "many animals," and although the most amazing sight is of the silverback gorilla family, you are apt to have the opportunity to trade eyebrows-up surprise with mole rats, hippos, and so on. The walking tour follows a predetermined path, but offers different encounters each time, again because of the species' various napping and eating hours. For some, you'll have to look carefully, because although they are all safely on the other side of barriers, they have no way of knowing that you are, too.

The Maharaja Jungle Trek is a similar living diorama, but featuring Indian and Southeast Asian animals, including Komodo dragons, antelope, and tigers. Along the way, you'll pass right through one of those wonderful old-fashioned aviaries, a combination giant-birdcage and lush, semitropical environment. Full-color pictures of the various bird species are available so you can identify what you're seeing, and "full color" doesn't begin to give a sense of the brilliant and ornate feathers on display here. The only disappointment is that you do have to keep moving, but at least it's rare that anybody really hurries you along.

The other often overlooked must-see is the Tree of Life itself, a 145-foot miracle of Imagineering that puts even the Swiss Family Robinson Treehouse in the shade. As tall as a 14-story office building, with a trunk 50 feet across and branches more than three times that, it's so hefty that it was modeled over a modified oil derrick. But that's not simple vine and bark you see gnarled around it: A whole corps of sculptors worked six days a week for two years to perfect the surface, a remarkable now-you-see-it, now-you-don't maze that fits animals, fish, birds, and insects together like ones of those children's puzzles magazines used to publish. Only this "maze" includes more than 350 creatures, and it's worth stopping four or five different times during the day to try to see them, because the shifting shadows of the moving sun reveal the cockatoo even as they seem to obscure the lion. Beautiful, moving, and almost humbling (ages of man cannot wither nor customary exploitation stale the animals' infinite variety), the Tree of Life is an accomplishment of a sort even the most playful Imagineer could take serious pride in—which may be why it is visible, like a monument, from so many other "elevated" places around Walt Disney World.

While you're wandering around the trails at the base of the Tree of Life, you'll discover another apparently unlikely best bet, *It's Tough to Be a Bug!* A second cousin to the popular *It's a Bug's Life* animated feature, it's actually the third of the super-3D attractions, this one with the extra visual assistance of computer-animated wizards from Pixar. Like *Honey, I Shrunk the Kids,* it includes a physical thrill or two, but it's nothing that will hurt or jolt you. In fact, although this is often passed off as a children's show, it delights everyone of every age who goes in. The waiting area is decorated with "broadway" and film posters promoting famous productions, albeit with new insectual twists. The whole theater is nice and cool, too.

Second Best

The only reason that the Dinosaur Jubilee is in a alternative class is that the Museum of Natural History in New York and other such larger collections, not to mention endless dinosaur movies and PBS shows, have made dinosaur skeletons almost commonplace. And also because many of the Disney bones are not actual fossil skeletons, but casts and reproductions. Still, they are fascinating in their sheer, cruel beauty; there's a prehistoric "fish" that is like sculpture, and it only takes a few minutes to walk through the exhibit if you aren't interested in reading the captions.

Even if it doesn't immediately catch your eye, stop as you walk past the Fossil Preparation Lab and consider what you're looking at. The bones being carefully removed from their stone and sand encasing are absolutely real—those of the 65-million-year-old *Tyrannosaurus rex* nicknamed "Sue," the largest complete *T. rex* skeleton ever uncovered, which was sold for $8.36 million at auction to the Field Museum of Natural History in Chicago. The laboratory exhibit at DinoLand U.S.A. is an actual branch of the Field institution. When the entire skeleton has been reassembled, one of two full-sized casts, the other a traveling version, will be on display at DinoLand U.S.A.

Similarly, depending on the show itself, the entertainment at the open-air Theater in the Wild can be a first or second choice; you'll have to read the program Tip Board.

Flights of Wonder is a nice trained-bird show, although it's gussied up and dumbed down by a fairly predictable script (but then, this is an all-ages show). There are some impressive hawks and such, and an owl or two, but whether these really grip you may have to do more with where you live and how active a bird-watcher you are. It's certainly restful and passive.

Don't Bother

Regretfully, although it's a great idea, the amount of veterinary work you see performed at Conservation Station, the amount of time you may have to spend waiting for the Wildlife Express to go there (and the brevity of the train ride after that), tend to make it a low-priority stop. The petting zoo is sweet, but not exactly rare (except that the particular species there are endangered); and if you happen to be a Hidden Mickeys initiate, you will definitely want to go. Perhaps now that Discovery Island, which also housed an animal medical facility, has been closed, the veterinary exhibit will be expanded, which would be wonderful, because it gives you a new perspective on the effort required to breed, deliver, maintain, and treat the hundreds of thousands of animals, birds, and fish in Disney World.

You can probably do without spending any time at Camp Minnie-Mickey or even crossing that bridge, unless you are just curious about the very old-fashioned summer-camp look of the place (Goofy fishin' with a pole), or are such a fan of *The Lion King* that you need to see this version as well as the multimedia show in Fantasyland. (Although admittedly, if you like the live re-creations of Disney movies that are all over the park, this is a very good one.)

Tips and Tales

The adult gorillas in the Pagnani Forest enclosure are named Hope and Gino. The bamboo that seems to be the only barrier between the spectators and the gorillas is actually Imagineered bamboo made of molded steel, and the seemingly shallow marsh is a much deeper chasm made to look innocent by extra-tall reeds.

The fossil imprints along the Cretaceous Trail are correct to the period, and include ancient forms of gingko trees and lizards as well as insects and simple animals.

Here's a time-saving tip: When you go to the Kilimanjaro Safaris entrance, look around carefully; sometimes the cast members are handing out time-specific tickets from a separate booth, meaning you can get in line at any time inside a 20- or 30-minute window. But this two-step process isn't always obvious, and ticketless visitors who get all the way to the first manned way-station are told they have to go back or wait in a secondary line. The mitigating news is that although the unticketed group isn't loaded on the cars at anything like the same rate as the first queue, they are in fact loaded, so you won't be locked out entirely.

Speaking of the safari vehicles, they are neither real Jeeps nor Humvees nor most of the other things people guess, but converted GMC trucks that run on propane.

Like Epcot's World Showcase, the Animal Kingdom is staffed ("cast," in the Disney jargon) by natives of countries being portrayed, both as participants and entertainers/artists; and they are singularly impressive attractions in their own rights. Don't miss the opportunity to make their acquaintance. Also, there are plenty of older greeters at Animal Kingdom who can tell you how tiring or pleasant particular rides or theaters are; you can trust their judgment.

Incidentally, the Animal Kingdom was originally supposed to include another section, one that showcases fantastical fictional creatures such as dragons, unicorns, and trolls. So far as we know, it's still on the drawing board, but one can only imagine that Imagineering technology like that which animates a *Carnotaurus,* if turned to lifting a Pegasus into flight, will be magical indeed.

Part Five

Sports and Recreation

You would be hard-pressed to come up with any sort of nonextreme recreational activity that is not available somewhere in Walt Disney World, with the possible except of bowling and the super slalom (and there are some surprisingly similar virtual effects available at Epcot and DisneyQuest). Otherwise, the World is your playground: golf, tennis, croquet, swimming, boating, fishing, skiing, ice skating, weight lifting, trail riding, rock climbing, running, volleyball, biking, parasailing, and scuba diving—even NASCAR driving. There's no official skateboard or inline skating areas, but none are necessary; there are sidewalks, parking lots, roads, and, though we hate to point it out, stairways everywhere.

However, we caution you that you should make as many reservations or tee times as you can as early as you can; consult the operator or hotel clerk when you call. Golf tee times can be made as far ahead as 60 days if you're staying at one of the resorts, or 30 days if you're staying outside; call (407) 939-4653. Or ask about Golf Getaway packages or other sports packages.

The Water Parks

The three Disney World water parks—the small and sweet River Country, the mixed smooth- and surf-water Typhoon Lagoon, and the 66-acre big bear, Blizzard Beach—aren't sporting arenas, exactly, although the idea of "skiing" barefoot at 60 miles an hour down 120 feet of water may constitute the thrill of victory and the agony of the feet.

River Country   The oldest of the three, built in 1976, River Country was intended to play on the Tom Sawyer family-film age-of-innocence theme that still dominated Disney planning at the time. It's also the least expensive: $17 if you don't have a pass that covers it, a good $10 or $12 less than the other two. It's an old-time swimming hole with (artificial) boulders for walls, waterfalls, rope swings, reasonably sedate "white-water rafts," and pretty white sand beaches. This can be the most relaxing of the three, because thrill seekers are more apt to look to the other two parks; on the other hand, parents of small, less experienced children sometimes retreat here, too. Bring a picnic if you like.

Typhoon Lagoon   Built nearly 20 years later and on a scale seven times the size, Typhoon Lagoon is far more of a playground than River Country, with a 100-foot-tall "mountain" that spews out water slides, "typhoon"-battered concession stands, geysers, and tube rides. Actually, whereas River Country is more an oversized swimming pool, Typhoon Lagoon is its own theme park, with a surf pool (that is, with machine-produced "tsunamis" higher than those at wave pools and designed for body surfing); a snorkeling area called Shark Reef stocked with smallish and nonthreatening hammerhead and leopard sharks among flocks of tropical fish (this is also visible through a viewing wall); and, to offset the 50-foot water slides through which swimmers usually barrel at about 30 miles an hour, there's a really relaxing tube ride that wanders for nearly a mile through a "rain forest" and assorted archaeological anomalies. The story behind the park is that it used to be a pleasant resort that was upended by, in quick order, a typhoon, an earthquake, and a volcanic eruption, which left a hapless shrimp boat marooned atop "Mount Mayday," where it periodically blows water out its stack like a beached whale. (Here's a tip for sun-bathers pursuing an even tan: The smokestack goes off every 30 minutes—time to turn over.)

Blizzard Beach   The newest, largest (66 acres, more than eight times the size of River Country), and most theatrical of the three, Blizzard Beach also has a full-blown (so to speak) history, though one with a logic only a Floridian could love. It seems that during an unusual cold snap that dumped a freak blanket of ice over the area, a real estate developer had the smart idea of making lemonade from lemons by opening a ski resort, complete with a little chalet and ski lifts; but of course, the climate eventually reverted, and the entire resort went into meltdown. The peak is called Mount Gushmore, and there are 17 water slides in all, counting raft rides, tube slides, and the infamous Summit Plummet, which measures about 350 feet, starts off with a 120-foot freefall at a 66° angle, and generates sliding speeds of about 60 mph. The "chicken slide" is only 90 feet long. (The view from the 120-foot chair ride to the peak is worth it even if you don't want to dare the chutes.) This, too, is a total theme park, with a lovely float creek called Cross Country, a mild wave pool, raft rides, and so on; not surprisingly, it's very popular with children. Gauge your volume tolerance level, too. One possible tactic is to go earlier in the day, when some families might be doing the main parks; or you could wait until later, say, mid- or late afternoon, and hope to hit peak nap time.

Incidentally, Disney cast members and water park veterans will tell you that unless you are planning on sticking to the more sedate rides and floats or improving your tan, make sure you wear a strong and stay-put bathing suit; the slides and flumes can expose you to more than just a new experience. And it shouldn't even require neck problems to make older visitors think twice about Summit Plummet; many people complain of being shaken up and bruised, especially on the buttocks, which is undoubtedly part of the fun for kids, but not, perhaps, for the rest of us.

OTHER WATER SPORTS

Water comes in a lot of forms in Walt Disney World—Bay Lake and Seven Seas Lagoon, Buena Vista Lagoon, the Fort Wilderness waterways, the Disney Village waterways and the Sassagoula River, Barefoot Bay, Crescent Lake, and so on—and not surprisingly, boating comes in nearly every variety imaginable, too, from jet-skis or mini-speedboats (you must be age 18 for these, and the water patrol pays close attention) to 20-foot pontoons for larger parties. There are also canopy boats, rowboats, canoes, sailboats, catamarans, speedboats, and kayaks—even outrigger canoes at the Polynesian. (These require at least five passengers, but unlike the others, they're free, perhaps because most amateurs are so clumsy in them that they provide entertainment for other visitors.) Nearly every resort hotel has some sort of craft available, and if not, they can show you where to go.

For those who would rather be chauffeured than steer themselves, there are charter boats and excursions that you can book in advance, either for private parties, fireworks viewing, or picnic lunches. Ask at the BoardWalk; Yacht and Beach Club resorts; Contemporary, Polynesian, and Grand Floridian hotels; or at Cap'n Jack's Marina at the Marketplace.

Bay Lake was originally stocked with 70,000 largemouth bass who've been cheerfully spawning ever since (many are in the 8- to 10-pound range) and you can pole-fish off Fort Wilderness, the BoardWalk, and the Marketplace; or you can try the equally well-stocked but shadier catfish "fishin' hole" at Dixie Landings. (Everything you catch should be thrown back, although Disney regulations have a loophole for those actually camping out or cooking for themselves; however, it's best to check with the guide before you go. Some particularly large fish may be mounted; again, ask the guide.) You can arrange fishing trips, usually about two hours long, on pontoons that leave from several of the resorts or from Cap'n Jack's. You can bring your tackle or use the on-board equipment. Most of these require reservations some time in advance; call (407) 828-2621.

If you don't mind spending $60 for about ten minutes' fantasy of flying, you can go parasailing over Bay Lake and see Cinderella Castle the way Tinkerbell does; reservations are required, call (407) 824-1000, ext. 3586. Water skiing can be arranged for about $100 an hour, which covers the boat, a driver-instructor, two to four skiers, and skis if you don't have your own, along with mini-surfboards and knee boards; make reservations at least 24 hours in advance, call (407) 824-2621, specifying pick-up at Wilderness Lodge, Fort Wilderness, Grand Floridian, Contemporary, or Polynesian resorts.

If you have a scuba diving certificate and about $150, you can take a half-hour dunk into The Living Seas; call (407) 939-8687. As for swimming—hello? This entire World was built on water, remember? There isn't a hotel on the place without its own beach, mini-water park, or variety of pools, lap pools, hot tubs, whirlpools, fountains, waterfalls, geysers. . . .

Golf and Tennis

More and more adults play golf or tennis on a regular basis, and some may find that even a short vacation makes them miss their match. But don't worry. Even if you didn't come prepared, Disney World is ready. You can rent a tennis racket or set of golf clubs, tog up in brand-name or souvenir sportswear, and even buy shoes to suit the surface in the respective pro shops.

If you want to go back home with a new shot, this is definitely the place. You can even get golf lessons from Gary Player's son Wayne or other PGA and LPGA pros and play any of five courses geared to your proficiency level. Not only can you get tennis lessons from a USTA pro, you can play him for your tuition money; take two out of three sets, and the lessons are free. (The usual fees are $20–25 for a half-hour or $40–50 for an hour.) You can play on clay courts at the Grand Floridian or on the ultra-state-of-the-art artificial surfaces (hydrogrid clay with buried irrigation) at the Contemporary Resort or the Disney Institute. You can even play all night on the 24-hour lighted courts at the Dolphin, which is even more fun because they're free after 6 p.m.

The Racquet Club at the Contemporary has six hydrogrid courts, all lighted, open from 8 a.m. to 8 p.m. During the summer, when tennis camps fill up the Racquet Club, there are only two courts reserved for resort guests between 10 a.m. and 4 p.m. For reservations (24 hours in advance), lessons, or video analysis, call (407) 824-3578.

The Disney Institute has four equally high-tech courts, video, lessons, partner-match services, and pro shop, but it goes even further: The Peter Burwash International school helped design the two-hour classes, but there are also some in-depth packages and half-exercise, half-lesson courses; call (407) 827-4455 for more information. To reserve a place in the two-hour program, call (407) 827-4800 (up to two weeks ahead of time).

Several of the other resorts, including BoardWalk, Old Key West, Yacht Club, and the Plaza hotels have courts as well; inquire when making reservations.

Disney has been known to promote its golf facilities by calling itself "The Magic Linkdom"; though corny, it's not inaccurate (which itself is typical of the market-savvy Disneyites). Its five championship courses, three of which are PGA tour facilities, have to stand up to more than 250,000 rounds of golf every year, along with nearly 400 tournaments. Greens fees on these are about $120 for resort guests.

If for some incomprehensible reason these aren't enough for you, call the Arnold Palmer Golf Academy at (407) 786-2429 or (800) 523-5999; you can also check the state-wide Tee Time network at (800) 374-8633; they can surely rustle up another course or two for you.

Disney World also has a 36-hole practice course where local pros work, called the Oak Trail Course, with greens fees of about $25 per round; there are also driving ranges and even miniature golf courses for less ambitious types. Fantasia Gardens is designed to resemble, as you might guess, scenes from *Fantasia,* including the hefty hippos and prima ballerina ostriches, tipping pails and walking brooms, and so on. Not only that, but there are surfaces and laser beams that react to passing balls with music, special effects, and pop-up scenery. It's more of a game than a golf course; but its sibling, Fantasia Fairways, is literally a mini-golf course, with miniature hills, greens, water traps, bunkers, and so on. Rounds are about $10; call (407) 560-8760.

Biking and Running

Although biking may seem more appealing to those with several days to explore Disney World or repeat visitors who'd like to see more of the nature side, it's a great way to see several of the prettiest resort areas. There are bikes for rent, sometimes tandem bikes, at the Disney Institute, Fort Wilderness, Wilderness Lodge, Port Orleans, Dixie Landings, Coronado Springs, BoardWalk, Old Key West, and Caribbean Beach. There are also four-wheeled surreys that are like covered bikes for rent across the BoardWalk marina. The routes range in length from about a mile around the BoardWalk to nine miles of path at Fort Wilderness. (Remember that most bike paths are also jogging and walking routes, and in some cases might have golf cart traffic as well.)

Running is obviously popular in a place with so much scenery (and sheer space); Disney World is now the site of a popular marathon that is run on a different course through the theme parks every January. If you're the sort of habitual runner who can't pass a week without a road race, call for local information at (407) 898-1313. For less ambitious joggers, there are maps available at each of the hotels that show the nearest trails and access points. Trails are usually no more than three miles long, but most are loops, so you can just go around again. The ones at Fort Wilderness and around the Disney Institute have fitness stations as well. And there are tracks at the Wide World of Sports that may be used if competitions are not under way.

Working Out and Other Exercise

Exercise clubs are more popular than ever, and as usual, Disney is right on the leading edge of the trend. Most of the hotels have health clubs, but they range from straightforward to state of the art; if yours doesn't have quite what you're looking for, the fancier fitness centers at the Grand Floridian, Contemporary, BoardWalk, and Disney Institute are open to all Disney World guests. The club at the Dolphin is the name-brand Body by Jake Health Studio, which admits travelers staying outside Disney World as well. All charge a fee, payable either by the day or length of stay, except for R.E.S.T. at Old Key West and the health club at the Swan, which are free to their own guests. (If you're brand-name conscious, the Disney Institute and Grand Floridian prefer Cybex, Body by Jake uses Polaris, and most of the rest are Nautilus-dependent.) Most of the clubs also have personal trainers and massage therapists available; check with the specific fitness club.

Scientists have recently figured out that dancing is great exercise. We already knew that. In any case, you have your choice of beats: 1940s retro, 1960s retro, 1970s retro, C&W, hip-hop, and so on, most of it at Pleasure Island. There, the settings are sometimes a little more cutting edge than the actual music. (After all, it is better to look good . . .) At Mannequins, for example, the look is technopop—quick-cut lighting effects, rotating dance floor, occasional professional dancer showcase—but the music is retropop. At 8TRAX, the look is urban rave, but the music is very 1970s, retro-kitsch pop, and disco. At BET SoundStage, the look is vaguely techno-warehouse, but the tunes are hip-hop, urban contemporary, and quiet storm. The others are more predictable. The Wildhorse Saloon, a joint venture with the Opryland folks who operate a similar Wildhorse in Nashville, is a C&W dance hall that draws mostly 20- and 30-somethings who prefer line-dancing to facing one another. The Rock & Roll Beach Club is also retro, but more classic rock and pop (yeah, surf music).

Over at the BoardWalk is the latest retro-trend to go very 1990s: big band and swing dance. Atlantic Dance does mostly classic swing with the occasional Latin swing change-up.

Among other sporting activities provided for at Disney World are croquet (courts at Port Orleans and the BoardWalk Resort), rock climbing (classes at the Disney Institute), and parasailing (the Contemporary marina). There are 45-minute trail rides around Fort Wilderness, but they're pretty much of a plod; call (407) 824-2832 to make reservations. The trail rides at the nearby Hyatt Grand Cypress Resort are a little more challenging; call (407) 239-1938.

There are volleyball courts, all for pick-up games, at a dozen locations; ask your hotel clerk for the nearest one. In cold weather, thanks to the recent craze for ice skating, Disney staffers pour the surface for a skating rink at the West Side. If you want to follow in Joe Montana's footsteps, you can play around at the NFL Experience at Disney's Wide World of Sports complex (see below).

If you're just into walking—and if you somehow don't feel as if you're getting enough of it around the theme parks—there are maps of trails around Fort Wilderness, Discovery Island, and Caribbean Beach available at the respective guest services counters, plus a nice nature trail inside River Country.

Disney's Wide World of Sports

Dough knows sports. That's putting it strongly, perhaps, but spectator sports are really big business, and over the past decade, the Disney Company has focused a remarkable portion of its attention and financial resources on the pro sports arena. In 1992, Disney paid $50 million for the NHL expansion team the Mighty Ducks. In 1995, Disney acquired the 24-hour ESPN sports cable network as part of its $19 billion deal for ABC/Capital Cities. In 1996, it paid an estimated $140 million for the American League's California Angels and $70 million toward the renovation of Anaheim Stadium (now Edison Field). In 1998, it spent more than $10 billion for the rights to broadcast NFL and college football, including the bowl games. Such investments require constant

---

Spa Pleasures

Disney World is full of fitness opportunities these days; but if your idea of a health club is a massage room or an aromatherapy tub, look no further. There are three full-service day spas at Disney World offering body wraps, hydromassage, reflexology, herbal scrubs, thalassotherapy, body polishing, manicures, pedicures, and so on: the Villas at the Disney Institute, the Spa at the Wyndham Palace, and the Grand Floridian's Spa and Health Club. Each offers half- and whole-day packages, à la carte spa services, even body-fat testing and nutritional counseling if you get inspired to body-consciousness.

However, if you don't really need lavender in your massage oil, most of the fitness centers in the resorts also have whirlpools, saunas or steam rooms, massages by appointment, and tanning booths.

---

reinforcement, such as the $80 million, six-year contract to Mo Vaughn. No wonder Disney World flashes the ESPN logo nearly as often as Mickey's ears.

So it was natural, in business terms at least, that Disney should play on one of ABC's most popular franchises by building the Wide World of Sports, a 100-million-dollar, 200-acre athletic complex from the designer of Oriole Park at Camden Yards, the Cleveland Indians' Jacobs Field, and the Ballpark at Arlington (Texas).

It includes a retro-ish 8,500-seat lighted baseball stadium where the Atlanta Braves train and play their home exhibition-season games, plus four major-league practice fields, 20 major-league pitcher's mounds, four softball fields, and eight batting tunnels. The 5,000-seat fieldhouse holds six basketball courts and a weight room and hosts dozens of competitions and clinics in fencing, wrestling, martial arts, badminton, racquetball, gymnastics, and even coaching and groundskeeping. There is an Olympic-quality track and field complex; and an Olympic-tested 250-meter velodrome that was disassembled after the 1996 Atlanta Olympics and moved to Disney World. It has four convertible fields suitable for football, rugby, soccer, field hockey, lacrosse, and so on; 12 tennis courts, including a 2,000-seat stadium center court where the U.S. Men's Clay Court Championships are played; and five outdoor sand volleyball courts.

In addition to the Braves, it is now home to perennial basketball faves the Harlem Globetrotters, the Basketball Hall of Fame (which puts on its Fantasy Camps at the facility), and, beginning in 1999, to the Senior Olympics. The complex was also designed to be the greatest permanent center for amateur athletics in the country, serving as headquarters of the Amateur Athletic Union (AAU), and will be hosting an increasing number of college competitions as well. An Olympic-sized pool and diving facility, and an ice hockey rink are on the drawing boards.

Even when nothing else is going on there, you can test your own punting/passing/kicking skills at the NFL Experience, which is a sort of playground with a football theme. (Just don't complain to us if you discover you're too old to be horsing around like that.)

To inquire about events there, call the Sports Line at (407) 363-6600. Many of these events do sell out, so you should try to call in advance.

Professional Sports Outside Disney World

The central Florida area is, of course, prime spring training territory; grapefruit league action could well be part of a Disney World vacation. Not only do the Atlanta Braves spend exhibition season at the Wide World of Sports, but the Houston Astros train at Osceola County Stadium in nearby Kissimmee, which is home to their A-league team, the Kissimmee Cobras (phone (407) 933-5500); the Kansas City Royals train at Baseball City Stadium in nearby Haines (phone (813) 424-2424); and the Orlando Rays, AA farm team for the Tampa Bay Devil Rays, play at Orlando's Tinker Field (phone (407) 649-7297).

The Orlando Arena is the other major sports facility in town, and it hosts, depending on the season, the NBA Orlando Magic (phone (407) 896-2442), the Orlando Predators arena football team (phone (407) 872-7362), and the minor-league ice hockey Solar Bears (phone (407) 872-7825). Magic games are usually sold out, but the arena has a cancellation window that opens about 90 minutes before game time, and you can probably get a seat unless it's playoff time.

Part Six

Nightlife

One measure of how much Walt Disney World has evolved since it was just a twinkle of fairy dust in Walt Disney's eye is the lengths to which it now goes to lure the party crowd. In addition to all the alcohol now sold in the parks (see "Part Eight: Drinking and Dining"), there are whole areas—mini-theme parks, in effect—devoted to keeping good-time money in Disney cash registers and, like the Disney Village Marketplace, of persuading Orlando residents to "visit" Disney World on a regular basis. Of course, there is a less exploitative way to look at it: Disney never wants its guests to feel bored or short-changed, even at 2 a.m. But it is certainly true that Pleasure Island, the biggest and most ruthlessly commercial of the nightlife areas, was created to siphon off some of the after-hours business that was then flocking to Church Street Station, the nightclub complex in downtown Orlando. Pleasure Island's success, and the likelihood that locals might come even more often if they didn't always have to pay for admission, certainly inspired the expansion into Disney's West Side.

For whatever reasons, once Disney had decided to go into the nightlife business, it did so with typical exuberance, determined to create whole "environments," re-creating a variety of eras, styles, and activities. Whatever your preferred amusement at home, you can probably find a fancier version here.

To put it in appropriately Disneyesque terms, Pleasure Island is the Papa Bear of adult playtime, Disney's West Side is the Mama Bear, and BoardWalk is the Baby Bear—but as to which fits you ju-u-u-u-st right depends on your personal style. We find most of Pleasure Island too programmed for pure relaxation, although that very programmatical, radio-band sort of variety is what appeals to many people. It is also partly laid out on a slant, which isn't always obvious and can mean that older visitors or those who have walking difficulties may find it uncomfortable; there's an outdoor dancing area; and the crowd tends to get increasingly boisterous as the night wears on. BoardWalk has a fresher look, but if you don't happen to be a good dancer or a sports fan, you will probably find it a little short of alternatives. The West Side is admittedly less participatory and more "performance" oriented, but it has the most even balance of nightclubs, restaurants, and shopping; it also has many places to sit down along the way.

Pleasure Island

At Pleasure Island, every night is New Year's Eve—without the headache of making good resolutions.

Pleasure Island is the most specifically adult theme park within Disney World, a giant block party with several thousand of your closest personal acquaintances. One admission price ($21) covers the entire complex of seven nightclubs, as well as assorted restaurants and souvenir shops. The shops and a few of the eateries open at 10 a.m. every day, and visitors to Disney Marketplace can wander through without paying; after 7 p.m., however, tickets or multipark passes and hand stamps are required. (Visitors or Disney guests who have been shopping all day and want to stash their haul before going club-hopping can rent lockers at most of the major nightclubs.)

But aside from needing your all-park pass or ticket, this isn't very much like a Disney attraction. In fact, only one of the clubs here, the **Adventurers' Club,** bears any resemblance to a Disney production in terms of cast members or even construction. So, if you're thinking it's another theme park in that sense, you'll have to readjust your expectations downward (though after midnight you might think of it as "Animal Kingdom II").

Alcohol is plentiful, but the controls are pretty strict. Adults (over age 21) are issued plastic ID bracelets that are nearly impossible to take off, even the next morning; without a bracelet, even with a gray beard, you won't get served. Guests under age 21 are admitted everywhere except the **Mannequins** disco, where the state-of-the-technopop lighting effects, rotating dance floor, occasional choreographed outbursts, and shifting mix-and-match crowd make it hard to monitor who's drinking what. (Avoiding teenagers isn't the only reason to go to Mannequins if you can really dance—Disney cast members, many of whom have substantial professional training, tend to hang out here after work.)

Each of the half a dozen music clubs on Pleasure Island offers a different style of music, just like the FM band of your car radio: You just sort of pick your favorite playlist: urban/hip-hop, golden oldies, country, jazz, and so on. And if you're really nostalgic for those *Solid Gold* dancers, you can hang around the outdoor stage at the end of town and wait for the "party" to get started.

Although it apparently came as something of a surprise to the American public and the general music press, at least before the 1999 Grammy Awards, a lot of yuppie suburban teens and 20-somethings are buying what used to be called "black urban" music, namely, R&B and hip-hop. The **BET SoundStage,** from the folks at Black Entertainment Television, looks sort of like a techno/house/warehouse/rave club, or maybe a hip-hop video stage set, with concrete on the floor and video screens on the walls. But the music isn't quite that cutting edge, except when the DJs and VJs, who are stationed with the bartenders on the mezzanine overlooking the dance floor, have so few clearly un-hip visitors to worry about that they can play what they really like.

The **Wildhorse Saloon,** a joint venture with the Opryland folks who operate a similar Wildhorse in Nashville, doesn't seem to have consulted with the Opryland stagehands—it doesn't have the swank or the strutting room of the original, though it's pleasant enough. It's a C&W dance hall that offers potent singles bar-style drinks (and a bit of barbecue-style noshing), free line-dance lessons several times a week, and sometimes live bands, mostly local, but occasionally national. It draws mostly 20- and 30-somethings.

So does **8 TRAX,** where the music is mostly golden oldies from the retro-hip 1970s, leaning heavily toward synth-kitsch pop and disco. (The name is the best joke here.) If you'd rather trip back a little farther, to the '60s and maybe even a bit beyond that, head to the **Rock & Roll Beach Club,** which is also retro, but more classic rock and pop (meaning back when "surf music" meant the

Beach Boys rather than Jimmy Buffett). And the outdoor **West End Stage,** which hosts local and regional (and Disney-staff) classic rock bands, can be infectiously cheery, but sometimes it feels like a not-too-successful frat-house reunion.

The **Pleasure Island Jazz Company** is pretty much what it sounds like: a smallish room with the classic exposed brick walls and pretty nice, sometimes very nice, blues and jazz by mostly local bands, with the occasional touring star. But this, too, is radio-tested stuff, quiet storm and easy-listening for the Kenny G generation.

The other two clubs are not music clubs but performance venues. The **Comedy Warehouse** is exactly what it sounds like, one of those half-improv, half-canned joke factories that were all the rage in the early '90s, where members of the audience supply names and details and the cast invents quickie songs about them. It's clever enough, but with these sorts of clubs, if you've seen one, you've seen them all. Of course, if you like one, you may like them all, too—depends on your sense of humor. And the whole club functions as a sort of warm-up show, because the first seating is at 7:15 p.m., whereas the other clubs don't open until 8. The Comedy Warehouse also has the lion's share of the Hidden Mickeys in Pleasure Island, which is another way to pass some time: To the right of the stage, for example, the bicycle wheel "head" has a clock and a drum for ears, the trampoline has two drum ears, and at the far left end of the room there's a snowman whose eyes touch his nose. And on the dock behind the warehouse on the way to Mannequins, there are three tires hanging in familiar order. (For an explanation of Hidden Mickeys, see "Part Nine: 'Hidden Mickeys' and Other Grown-Up Games.")

The shows at the **Adventurers Club** are actually more elaborate and theatrically demanding than those at the Comedy Warehouse, because the "characters" are so over-the-top and vaudevillian. The concept is that this is one of those old explorers' clubs from the late 19th and early 20th centuries, half old London men's club and half Ripley's Believe-It-or-Not! trophy room. It's a little like a drinking man's Haunted Mansion: shrunken heads, sonorous butlers, macabre-comic souvenir cases, and photos of "members." Invisible ghostly hands play the piano in the library bar, and a rather tawdry music-hall "gypsy" heads up a little vaudeville revue. (Or, if it's around Christmas, there may be an old-fashioned "radio broadcast" that could pass as Garrison Keillor's worst nightmare.) There are costumed cast members wandering through the club, inducting new members into the secret hand- shake and the members' special greeting, "Kungaloosh!" And there are a half-dozen different shows, each of which last a half-hour or maybe 45 minutes, scheduled through the evening.

There's more to see than meets the eye here, which is just the point: The mezzanine, which circles the room and offers a good view of the main hall below, is full of joke memorabilia. The jokes here can be rather subtle, like the giant pharaoh's head that makes up one of the "stone" walls of the entrance (remember all those mummy's curses about entering tombs?), or cartoonish, like the casting rod in the hands of the classic statue of Poseidon in the center of the room. (The Adventurers Club also has a few Hidden Mickeys around: Look at the "fallen" checkers on the far book- shelf of the library.)

The clocks are on Disney time at Pleasure Island, so that the nightly "New Year's Eve" fireworks and "Auld Lang Syne" sing- along don't start until about 1:30 a.m. (Watch the three spotlights overhead; they'll touch periodically into another Hidden Mickey, visible from a long way away. And as you leave, look up at the Pleasure Island sign and consider Jessica Rabbit's quite pneumatic torso and her equally expansive hips.)

Disney's West Side

The West Side is the closest thing Disney World has to a real "downtown": movie theaters; a couple of live performance venues, including a state-of-the-art theatrical facility; a handful of restau- rants, some of them quite good; a little shopping, and so on. Like Pleasure Island, Disney's West Side adjoins Disney Marketplace, with its huge, free parking lot (and boat and bus transportation within the resorts); but unlike Pleasure Island, the West Side is always open to the public, though individual venues may charge admission.

The West Side, which caters to locals as well as tourists, is stud- ded with name-brand restaurant franchises. There's a **Planet Hollywood,** which is as much (or more) like another memora- bilia shop as a restaurant. There are occasional celebrity sightings there, but nothing really "entertaining." The food is the same as it is at any Planet Hollywood, meaning hefty and a little cute (i.e.,

Cajun pizza)—which is something of a puzzle, because surely no owners as body-conscious as Bruce Willis, Demi Moore, Sly Stallone, and Arnold Schwarzenegger could possible fit this stuff into their diets. The roadhouse-style **House of Blues** is both a restaurant and a music club; it's partly owned by "Blues Brother" Dan Aykroyd, but is New Orleans- rather than Chicago-style in decor, musical taste, and menu. If there's a name band playing in the club, you'll have to buy a ticket, but if it's just a local or DJ that night, or if you just want to sit in the restaurant, there's no cover. And the food is about as good as mass-produced Cajun/ Creole gets, though a little salty (which it also is in New Orleans).

The **Wolfgang Puck Cafe** is like a miniature of Puck's many culinary ventures, in that its various floors mix and match his upscale, more casual, and even fashion menus; you got your "gourmet pizza," you got your California sushi, and you got your pastas. Gloria Estefan's **Bongos Cafe** is more like a franchised Cuban restaurant than a serious bar—in fact, considering the wealth of Latino restaurants in Florida, a somewhat disappointing one—though the outside seating can be nice.

Two of the better restaurants in Disney World are also on the West Side, **Fulton's Crab House** and the **Portobello Yacht Club,** both of which are actually operated by the very successful Levy Restaurants group out of Chicago. Fulton's, which is absolutely huge (it seats 700 at a time) and which should be far more frantic than it ever is, is a three-decker paddle-wheeler moored off Pleasure Island (the former *Empress Lilly,* named for Walt's wife). It specializes in crab, from Dungeness to Alaskan king (an appetizer of fresh stone crab claws and a glass of wine at the rear deck bar are sunset heaven), oysters, grilled fish of the day, and so on, and it has a good and considered domestic wine list. Portobello's, which is just across the walkway, is Northern Italian, with some really good thin-crust pizzas (some people prefer them to Puck's), pastas, veal, and so on. Its wine list, mostly Italian, of course, is also good.

The West Side has an **All-Star Gear** store, a **Virgin Megastore,** the now-requisite cigar store, the neo-Zen shop, **Starabilia** (another of those celebrity-gilt-by-association boutiques), and so on. (For a description of these and other stores in the West Side, see "Part Ten: Shopping in Walt Disney World.")

The West Side also houses the five-story **DisneyQuest,** a sort of virtual-reality theme park with interactive computer games, "time travel," space wars, and so on. Twenty-somethings may find this irresistible, though older visitors may not find it so appealing to kill an evening (and another admission price) leaning over yet another computer screen.

As if to emphasize the fact that Disney is back in the movie business, the 24-screen **AMC cineplex** near the parking lot entrance is definitely state-of-the-sales-art, equipped with the George Lucas-designed THX supersound system, stadium seating in two-thirds of the cinemas, and even a couple with old-fashioned balconies and double-height screens.

But the most impressive attraction on the West Side, and the one that not coincidentally sits at the end of the street like a real-life Cinderella Castle, is the high, white, and handsome theatrical palace that is now the permanent home of **Cirque du Soleil,** the Montreal-based acrobatic troupe that has revolutionized modern circus entertainment. The theater is designed to suggest both a castle and an old-fashioned tent, with multiple "peaks" under which technicians (and where else could you find better engineers than in Disney World?) have created a fantastic array of rigging, sound and light equipment, hooks, and hideaways. Inside, its steeply raked seating makes for (nearly) perfect views of every act; the built-in trampolines, elevated stage sections, orchestra balconies, and multilevel trapezes return "tumbling" to high theater.

Even with its quite serious ticket prices—$56.50 for ages ten and up, $44 for kids age three up to age nine—it is guaranteed to be a huge success. Anyone who has ever seen a performance by one of the Cirque companies (there are now several) or its alumni spinoffs, such as Cirque Eloise, knows that it is gripping, thrilling, mysterious, enigmatic, funny, exhilarating . . . addictive. Even though the shows do not change very often (after all, they take months to conceive, design, stage, choreograph, and score, not to mention training and recruiting), fans return repeatedly. And with the constantly changing Disney World population, they will easily fill ten shows a week.

The BoardWalk

If Pleasure Island is an adult playground and the West Side an ideal cultural center, the BoardWalk is a little bit like a costume party where the hosts hope you'll dance, but have left the championship fight on the big-screen TV in the rec room just in case you won't (and who stocked beer as well as champagne).

Unlike Pleasure Island or the West Side, which are entirely commercial complexes, the BoardWalk is half resort, half theme park: The hotel is built right over the entertainment and shopping strip, and the theme is the Atlantic City/Long Island resorts of the 1930s. (There is no park pass or ticket required, but as at Disney's West Side, some attractions charge their own covers.) Of the three, it seems to draw the oldest crowd, at least on a repeat basis; it's certainly more comfortable for tired or weak legs than Pleasure Island, and its proximity to Epcot means you can view the fireworks a lot earlier. On the other hand, it also gets a fair amount of 20-somethings, who are big on the big-band revival; and though the clubs are adults-only, the resort gets a lot of families that may mean inline skating along the boardwalk.

The main entertainment venue is an elaborate big band-era dance hall called **Atlantic Dance,** which plays the martini-lounge nostalgia theme to the hilt with a ceiling glittering with mirror balls, marble bars, a bandstand, a grand staircase, a balcony to retire to between jitterbugs (and where you can nuzzle in love seats), and terraces to take in the fireworks. It even opens on to the terraces with the sort of French doors the dancers in movies used to step through into the garden. There is a short list of cocktail-party food (and, perhaps inevitably, cigars for sale). This is adults-only territory, and it's become fairly popular with local residents and the new generation of fairly serious dancers; most nights there's a quick dance lesson included for novices.

For the non-dancers in the party, the BoardWalk has a comedy-music bar called **Jellyrolls,** which like the Comedy Warehouse at Pleasure Island, opens early to warm up the crowd. It's a sort of "Dueling Banjos" on ivory, with two pianos, two players, and a lot of shouted encouragement. Despite the name, which suggests jazz, the music tends to the classic rock variety (again), but that does mean the patrons are sometimes lured into singing along. (Since this also gets some local residents, it occasionally seems like karaoke night at the VFW.) Jellyrolls is supposed to look like a speakeasy or roadhouse, warehousy and with stools pushed up against the walls.

For the non-martini crowd, there's the **Big River Grille & Brewing Works,** which is a pleasant little cafe, but the bar itself is quite small, unfortunately for those who like to talk brewing with the staff; also the "stools" are a little weird, as if they were bought from a fire sale at a farm-equipment warehouse—something between a thresher seat and a shovel. The four or five beers brewed on premises are good to very good. (Some of it is cask-conditioned, but it's not made much of; you have to know to ask about it.) It's a nice place to watch a sports event in the relative quiet of a regular bar, with only two regular-sized televisions. The food sounds better than it is, generally speaking, but no worse than most pubs.

Relative quiet, that is, because the real "recreation room" of the resort, which seats 220 in the "den," is **ESPN Club,** a sports center and macho-sandwich bar with maxi-screen TVs, another 75 regular screens, eight Internet hookups, a real broadcasting radio station, constantly updated scores and odds, and, in case you get inspired, interactive sports games and virtual-reality pods. You don't even have to worry about missing a crucial point during your personal breakaway; the rest rooms are equipped with 14 monitors.

Foodwise, the BoardWalk restaurants also seem to split between the retro-sophisticates and the two-handed eaters. The **Flying Fish Cafe** is a trendy exhibition-kitchen seafood grill with copper detailing, daily-catch specials, veggie platters, champagne by the glass, hissing espresso machine, and so on. This, like Fulton's, is one of the better restaurants around, which may say something about the availability of good seafood in Orlando, but here it's a little gussied up—the grilled tuna is crusted with coriander, the snapper in potato wrap, and so on. It's the California grill in Florida disguise. **Spoodles,** on the other hand, mixes tapas, the trendy term for expensive snack foods, and pizza—food designed for more boisterous parties and, in the long run, bigger appetites, because it's hard not to order a lot of little plates. (Some of the seafood dishes, incidentally, resemble the Flying Fish recipes but are a little cheaper, so it needn't be a second choice.)

Part Seven

Adult Education

One of the things Walt Disney World executives realized in the late 1980s and early 1990s was that as the age range of Disney's audience expanded, so did their interests. Once its adult patrons were primarily parents resigned to child-oriented rides and amusements, but the raised-on-Disney generations now include professionals and DINKS (dual-income couples with no kids), pre-nesters and empty-nesters, retirees, entrepreneurs, and—now that Disney World has expanded far beyond the Magic Kingdom— visitors simply drawn to Disney World's more sophisticated attractions for their own sake. Plus the thrill-seekers and golfers, of course.

For those attuned to the market trends of popular culture, there were plenty of clues to the willingness of American adults in particular to learn new hobbies and skills. The explosion of interest in gourmet cooking magazines and TV shows, including a whole cable channel devoted to food; increasingly sophisticated versions of travel and leisure publications (and the craze for extreme travel); do-it-yourself programs, from "This Old House" to Martha Stewart; the development of ever more expensive and elaborate sports equipment such as tennis racquets and golf clubs, and even the invention of new sports; and, of course, the advent of the Internet all combined to expand the traditional "recreational" universe in unprecedented ways.

Medical advances extended life expectancies and improved the quality of life for middle-age and older adults. Competition among airlines and bus lines made travel not only cheaper but also more impulsive and frequent. Continued economic prosperity opened new doors, too. Retirement became the opportunity to travel, take on new hobbies, start small businesses or second careers, or go back to school altogether. In movies, TV shows, and even advertisements, older adults were being portrayed as sexy, smart, versatile, and open to experience—and, like the chicken and the egg, the image and the reality reinforced each other.

It isn't just a matter of vacation time, either. As more executives found it increasingly hard to get away for the once-traditional two weeks at a time (and to relax when they did get away), they began to look for long weekends that were intellectually stimulating and personally fulfilling—life-enhancing as well as professionally reinforcing. Some were interested in acquiring work-related skills, such as photography or desktop publishing. Some desired to learn the sort of personal skills that might come in handy in business entertainment—wine tasting, gourmet cooking, and so on—as well as ultimately enriching their retirement. For those who became health-conscious, new forms of sports and exercise beckoned along with new nutritional and culinary interests. They wanted to live, and they wanted to learn.

And they wanted to have fun, of course.

The Disney Institute

Disney CEO Michael Eisner began a private self-education course in self-improvement. He visited Chatauqua, the small New York town whose famous series of educational and cultural events in the late nineteenth century provided the personal edification of its residents and eventually became the basis of a sort of informal annual tour of the Northeast and mid-Atlantic resorts. Eisner was already aware of the increasing popularity of the Elderhostel network, which offers inexpensive educational vacations for senior citizens at colleges and universities worldwide. He decided that Walt Disney World was the perfect place to construct the new Chatauqua, a mini-campus where patrons could learn, enjoy, and enhance their lives in a resort atmosphere with all the amenities.

The Institute, which opened in early 1996, is probably the most purely adult "amusement" area in the entire Walt Disney World complex. It offers visitors the opportunities to perfect skills, plan new personal routines, revive old dreams, or just play around. It offers classes in what you might call home studies (a variety of cooking and wine classes, entertaining tips, organic gardening and hydroponics, topiary, interior design, gift-making, antiquing and faux antiquing), performing arts (storytelling, improvisation, script writing, stand-up comedy, theatrical makeup), media studies (radio DJing or reporting, TV production), sports and health (rock climbing and personal training sessions, dance, tennis, and golf), personal improvement (style and image counseling, money management, meditation), and even Disney specialties such as animation, claymation, computer animation, coloring, and sound mixing.

For the busy executive, there are classes in Web site construction, video and still photography, digital manipulation, and desktop publishing—all in well-considered, pleasant, and effective two- or three-hour segments. "The people who take our courses are professionals, and it's important that we don't waste their time," Disney Institute computer instructor Karen Nelson Sinibaldi told *Time* magazine. Which means you can design a new home page before lunch and get someone to correct your hook in the afternoon. It also means that the ingredients for the cooking classes are already washed for the most part, and somebody else does the dishes while you eat the results.

In addition to some 80 possible courses, the Institute campus includes two major performing arts venues, an indoor recital hall and an outdoor amphitheater that hosts dance troupes, acting companies, and musical concerts; plus a very up-to-the-moment health spa and all the body and soul tenders any visitor could have read about in any of those improvement magazines. Institute residents can start the morning with nature walks and t'ai chi sessions, take their courses during the day, and then enjoy prominent speakers and performing artists from all disciplines— Eugenia Zukerman, Pilobolus, Henry Louis Gates Jr.—in the evening hours. (These evening programs, incidentally, are open to all Disney World visitors; dinner and performance packages cost about $35, and since dinner is at Seasons, one of the nicer restaurants in the entire park, they are big-ticket events at small-ticket prices.)

Generally, Institute guests stay three or four days, although there are week-long packages and even special day services for Florida residents. A three-day stay with all meals, events, and one day's pass to a theme park starts at about $660 a day, double occupancy; although we say again, if you're going to take any cooking classes, you won't want to eat much outside of school. Without meals, packages start at $530. Big-name food and wine and garden design magazines frequently co-sponsor special seminars for intensive study. For more information on the Institute's programs, call (800) 282-9282. For more on Institute accommodations, see "Part Two: Where to Stay."

"Curiouser and Curiouser": Behind the Scenes

Curiosity is built into the human character. We want to know what makes things tick; so the very perfection of Disney's fantastic facades drive us to ask, How'd they do that? We want to enjoy the illusion and penetrate it at the same time—project ourselves into the scene, as it were (and in some cases, get our feet wet). Sometimes, especially with the education areas of Epcot, we want to know more, get closer, and take a little of the Disney experience back home.

There are dozens of behind-the-scenes tours and educational seminars conducted around the various theme parks, such as those that let guests in on the customs, taboos, and architectural references in Epcot's World Showcase (Hidden Treasures and Disney by Design); landscaping (Planting Ideas, Gardens of the World); film and animation (Inside Animation and Art Magic); or the machinery behind the magic (Innovation in Action, Keys to the Kingdom). Some of the tours concentrate on only one park and some move among several. Most have limited space and are offered only on certain days of the week. The best way to find out about your options is to call (407) WDW-TOUR in advance and ask about the kind of tours you're interested in.

For instance, one of the most popular tours is Backstage Magic, which takes seven hours and costs $185 on top of the park admission. (Make reservations early; space is limited.) Among highlights are examinations of the backstage computer systems at Body Wars and a second, varied location such as *American Adventure*; hands-on animation classes at Disney Studios, where lunch is served; a close encounter with the manatee environment at Living Seas, and the usual surprises. The somewhat cut-down version is called Keys to the Kingdom, which leaves from City Hall at 10 a.m. and sticks to the Magic Kingdom park, but spends a lot of time in the "Utilidor" and underground tunnels and includes some quick turns on Pirates of the Caribbean, The Haunted Mansion, and so on. It's best to make advance reservations, but you can check at City Hall in case there's still space (4.5 hours; $45 plus food).

One of the hot new tours is the Backstage Safari at Animal Kingdom, a three-hour look at the veterinary hospital, the stables and housing, warehouses, and so on ($60 plus park admission).

Visitors impressed with the various formal and foreign gardens at Epcot can take the Behind the Greens or the Gardens of the World tours by signing up at the Epcot entrance (each cost $45 in addition to park admission). A broader tour of the various tropical-style plantings ranges from Polynesian Village to Animal Kingdom to Adventureland; these weekend tours also cost $45 plus Epcot admission.

Those more intrigued by the architecture and culture of the World Showcase exhibits should look into the Hidden Treasures of Epcot tours, one that looks to the West and one to the East—but that refers to the lagoon, not the hemispheres, using *American Adventure* as the midpoint ($35 plus admission). Each half-World tour takes a couple of hours, or you can take in the entire circuit, stopping for lunch at Marrakesh; that will cost you $85 plus park admission and about five hours of your day.

The architectural design of the park and the Imagineers' almost compulsive attention to detail is covered in Disney's Architecture ($45). The architectural "theming" of the Walt Disney World complex as a whole is covered in Disney by Design, which includes such doubly behind-the-scenes structures as Disney Casting and the Team Disney offices (which will give you a very rare opportunity to see the somewhat abstract Hidden Mickey over the entrance to the driveway), Pleasure Island, Epcot, and some of the resorts. This has to be arranged in advance for a minimum of 15 people, though, so either scrounge some friends together or call about being put into a waiting list ($60, about 3.5 hours).

A less well-known tour is the Legends of the Magic Kingdom, an unadvertised jaunt ($35) that leaves about 7 a.m. from the Wilderness Lodge; a guide takes you to the park before opening and explains how the facades affect the apparent perspective of the park, shows the tunnels below and behind ground, and even exposes some Hidden Mickeys (see "Part Nine: 'Hidden Mickeys' and Other Grown-Up Games"). It's a rare chance to ask direct questions about the park, but you have to leave when the park opens to the public and return to Wilderness Lodge. Ask at the lodge guest services desk about this tour.

Epcot's D.E.E.P. training is short for Dolphin Exploration and Education Program, in which participants become guest researchers in actual studies; space is very limited for this class, which starts at 8:45 a.m. and goes until lunchtime ($45). If you have scuba diving certification, you can enroll in DiveQuest, which lets you visit among the tropical fish of the Living Seas ($140, all equipment provided).

There are also various animation classes, more gardening tips, and so on. If you have a particular interest not otherwise covered, you can arrange your own VIP Tour lasting anywhere from three to eight hours (you have to add in lunch at one of the full-service restaurants for the longer tours, but why not?). To arrange an individualized tour, call Disney Special Activities at (407) 560-6233 at least three days in advance and expect to pay $65 a hour plus any park admissions.

One last new group of classes, but of an entirely different sort, are the Richard Petty Driving Experience courses at the WDW Speedway, where you can either take a quick ride in the passenger seat of a stock car ($90), drive yourself for eight laps ($330), or work your way up to three ten-lap sessions ($1,100). All these include safety classes and background instructions first, of course. For these programs, call (800) BE-PETTY (237-3889).

Part Eight

Drinking and Dining

A few years ago, you could have joked that a chapter about drinking and dining in Walt Disney World was an oxymoron—and that still has a sting of truth about it. Whatever else it is (and it is many wonderful things), Disney World is no gourmet paradise. For the most part, in fact, the restaurants are as much "entertainment" as the rest of Disney World: The fast food joints get character decor and the international pavilions get native costumes.

Some restaurants seem to be extensions of the theme parks, like the Rainforest Cafes in Animal Kingdom and the Disney Village Marketplace, which have their own Audio-Animatronic elephants (which is really more reminiscent of Adventureland because the Animal Kingdom has live pachyderms). Sometimes it's even harder to tell the live entertainment and the dinner apart—for example, at the Coral Reef restaurant in The Living Sea, where some 6,000 sea creatures, including close relatives of those on the menu, are swimming around and around the glass wall of the dining room, trying to make you feel guilty. Nearly all the restaurants in the various resorts are extensions of the resort theme: Cajun at Port Orleans, New England clambake at the Beach Club, Floribbean at the Old Key West, and so on.

All in all, there are only a handful of places out of nearly 75 full-service restaurants that you could recommend for a special night out, or that have first-class wine lists suitable for business entertaining.

On the other hand, if the average guest at Walt Disney World were primarily concerned with pleasing his or her palate, the hottest dinner ticket at the park would not be the *Hoop-Dee-Doo Revue.* In fact, if you want to know what Disney World visitors really like, look at the numbers: Every day, they consume 1.3 million barbecued turkey legs, 7 million hamburgers, 5 million hot dogs, 46 million sodas, and 130 tons of popcorn.

So, for most people, food is a secondary consideration, and we don't want to belabor the point. This is not a critical evaluation of the restaurants in Disney World, but an overview of the choices. We're not leaving you totally clueless, of course: If you are looking for a place to have a really special meal, refer to the section on "'That's Amore': The Most Romantic Restaurants" in "Part Three: Romance in 'the World'" for recommendations. If you intend to make dinner part of an entire evening out, be sure to look back over "Part Six: Nightlife," with its lineup of restaurants in the West End and BoardWalk areas. And if you do care more about dining out on your vacation or would like to experiment with different cuisines, *The Unofficial Guide to Walt Disney World,* referred to in the introduction, includes in-depth reviews not only of the sit-down establishments in Disney World itself but also some of the better restaurants in Orlando.

One thing older adults (and international travelers) should be aware of is that most restaurants at Walt Disney World serve very substantial portions. You can easily put aside parts of dinners for lunches the next day if you have a refrigerator in your room; split an entree or load up at lunch and go light on dinner.

One other thing to note is that whatever you think of the cooking, the standards for purchasing groceries, food storage, and sanitary preparation are extremely high throughout Disney World, and you are a lot more likely to give yourself a little 24-hour "bug" from careless cooking that any Disney chef is.

As to drinking in Disney World, happily, opportunities abound, not only to find your "usual" cocktail but to maintain any trend habits you may have, from microbrewed beer to flights of fancy champagne. And you don't even have to finish your drink before hitting the park promenades, either: Many are cash and carry. Just be careful in a crowd, or you may be wearing that cocktail for the rest of the day.

"Pink Elephants on Parade": Bellying Up to the Bar(s)

Back when Walt Disney was scouting locations for his second theme park, he was invited by the business leaders of St. Louis, Missouri, to put it there; he turned them down flat after he discovered that the Busch family naturally expected to be selling their beer in his park once it opened.

Well, Walt may not quite be turning over in his grave—there is still no alcohol sold in the Magic Kingdom—but he could almost be floating in it, because it's available everywhere else. In fact, Epcot's World Showcase could function as an international bar crawl . . . and probably has. (If you're planning to test this theory, please appoint a designated director first.)

Once the Disney company realized that there was more money to be made in the adult trade than from even the most loyal kid, and that after all kids do grow up, it became a major part of its strategy to attract and entertain the over-age-21 market. In fact, as we pointed out in the introduction, the senior segment of Disney visitors is one of its most valuable and fastest growing. So, adults who are traveling without children, even temporarily, may feel a lot freer to take advantage of the many sociable situations. Let's face it: Alcohol tends to make price tags look smaller, appetites larger, and spirits higher, so why wouldn't Disney make them available?

Because it is the most specifically child-friendly park, the Magic Kingdom has so far resisted the temptation to offer Cinderella cocktails or fruit and rum drinks at the Tiki Room in Adventureland. But it's just about the only dry spot in town. At Epcot, both sit-down restaurants (the Coral Reef inside the Living Seas pavilion and the Garden Grill at The Land) offer alcohol; once you cross into World Showcase, you can drink as you promenade as boldly as if you were on Bourbon Street in New Orleans.

The fun here is that each pavilion serves beer produced in its home country; so although none are labels so rare you couldn't get them at a good liquor store, you can have a lot of fun comparing styles. Hosting a "progressive tasting" might be an unusual idea for business or wedding entertaining.

As you work your way around the lagoon, you have LaBatt's and Molson's at Le Cellier Steakhouse in the Canada pavilion;

Bass Ale and Guinness Stout on tap at the Rose & Crown Pub in the United Kingdom (don't get into a political argument about Irish self-rule, please, it's very rude); various French and Alsatian brands at Bistro de Paris and Chefs de France; Kirin at the Japanese Matsu No Ma; French at the Marrakesh restaurant in Morocco; Samuel Adams at The American Adventure; Beck's (in 33-ounce steins!) in the German Biergarten; Ringnes in the Restaurant Akershus in Norway; Tsing Tao in China; and Tecate and Dos Equis on draft in Mexico's Cantina de San Angel.

All these restaurants also have wines for sale; the German and French pavilions sell wines by the glass. Matsu No Ma and Tempura Kiku have plum wine and sake, and the Akershus buffet in the Norway pavilion has aquavit. Most of them, except L'Originale Alfredo di Roma and Le Cellier, also serve alcoholic spirits (and those that don't often have a national liqueur or house cocktail). And some, including France and Great Britain, have outdoor wine and beer sales, so you don't even have to slow your stride.

At MGM, you'll find a full bar at the '50s Prime Time Cafe, the Sci-Fi Dine-In Theater, the Catwalk Bar (a hideaway atop the Soundstage Restaurant), and the Hollywood Brown Derby. Mama Melrose's has beer, wine, and a liqueur or two; the Hollywood & Vine cafeteria has beer and wine. Cap'n Jack's Oyster Bar and the Rainforest Cafe in Disney Village Marketplace will keep you fully lubricated during your long, hot day of shopping. In the Animal Kingdom, you'll find the Dawa Bar just as you cross into Harambe and the other, larger Rainforest Cafe Bar just inside the front entrance.

If you prefer your beer with a more local label—very local, and preferably preservative free—Disney World can oblige with a raft of microbrews. The most prominent site, of course, is Disney's own brew pub, the Big River Grille & Brewworks on the BoardWalk, which produces five seasonal recipes in copper vats visible from the bar. There are also custom-brewed house labels at the Territory Lounge in Wilderness Lodge, Outer Rim at the Contemporary, Fulton's Crab House outside Pleasure Island, and Harry's Safari Bar at the Dolphin (which has those yard-long glasses that are so much fun the first time). The Crew's Cup Lounge at the Yacht Club has three dozen beers; the Laughing Kookabura at the Wyndham Palace has nearly a hundred.

You can also pursue the "ethnic" or regional flavor game in the resort restaurants, ordering Dixie Blackened Voodoo Lager at Bonfamille's in Port Orleans and Kirin or Sapporo at Kimono's in the Swan. And, in a bow to new Southwest chic, Juan & Only's Bar in the Dolphin stocks a list of rare and aged tequilas.

Disney World has also come a very long way in terms of wine sales. In addition to the more ordinary wines lists at most of the restaurants, it has a couple of very notable wine cellars, most famously perhaps at the California Grill atop the Contemporary Resort, which has a very smart all-domestic wine list (and a free wine-advice service; call (407) 824-1576 any time between noon and 10 p.m.). If you've just discovered the Northwest territory wines, try the Artist Point atop the Wilderness Lodge.

Victoria and Albert's in the Grand Floridian has a wine list to match its menu, and its prices. At Arthur's 27 restaurant in the Wyndham Palace—so named because the atrium is 27 stories high and the restaurant is at the top—the private dining room, which holds up to 12 people, is really the wine "cellar," with 800 bottles on display. Most of them can be ordered, and quite a few sampled in flights, at its Top of the Palace lounge. Martha's Vineyard Lounge at the Beach Club, like the big wine bars in New York and Los Angeles, also offers almost any of its wines in two-ounce flights.

Even in the theme parks, you can do pretty well: The Bistro de Paris and Chefs de France have a very good list (French, of course); the Hollywood Brown Derby has expanded its vintage California list; the lists at Fulton's Fish Market and the Portobello Yacht Club, both outside Pleasure Island, are very good, perhaps thanks to the purchasing leverage of Levy Restaurants; and David Copperfield's Magic Underground near Disney-MGM Studios, which is experimenting with an eclectic Los Angeles–New York sort of menu, is also working a little magic on the wine list.

This doesn't mean you can't find those cute "tropical" drinks if you want them. The Tambu Lounge at the Polynesian Resort and the Dawa Bar in Harambe Marketplace, just to name two, have cocktails the colors of the rainbow. Make sure you don't turn the same colors—those things aren't as innocent as they look, especially on a hot day.

The Five Mouse-ka-Beers

At the Big River Grille & Brewworks on the BoardWalk, you can sample five microbrews crafted on World premesis in the huge copper vats visible from the bar. While Walt might blush at the thought of such licentiousness, we think the "homebrewed" beer here is generally pretty good. They are all preservative free, with four standards available all the time and at least one brew that changes seasonally. There may be bigger beers served in "the World" and there may be more exotic beers, too, but there's something about a beer brewed on the mouse's turf that makes it seem, well, a bit magical.

"A Spoonful of Sugar": Flavors around "the World"

As you've undoubtedly noticed by now, Disney World is a trend-savvy place, and every market share has its niche. So if you've become habituated to wood-fired pizza (Palio in the Swan, the California Grill atop the Contemporary Resort, Mama Melrose's at MGM Studios, Portobello Yacht Club at Pleasure Island), espresso (the Starring Rolls Bakery at MGM Studios, Kusafiri Coffee Shop in Harambe, Forty-Thirst Street on the West Side, and the Fountain View at Epcot), or all-you-can-eat ('Ohana at the Polynesian, Chef Mickey's in the Contemporary, the Crystal Palace at the Magic Kingdom, Cape May Cafe at the Beach Club, 1900 Park Fare in the Grand Floridian), you can find a home here.

But Disney World is also about stars, about fantasies, and about meeting characters; the restaurant lineup is beginning to sound as much like a movie cast as the character meals at Cinderella's Royal Table.

The Planet Hollywood at Pleasure Island famously belongs to and has memorabilia from the likes of Demi Moore, Bruce Willis, and Sylvester Stallone (and, since this branch of the chain really looks like a planet, it becomes the "globe" entrance that matches

Epcot's Spaceship Earth, which just goes to show you how big an attraction it is). The West Side has two other celebrity-connected restaurant-nightclubs: the House of Blues, a New Orleans–style nightspot partly owned by surviving Blues Brother Dan Aykroyd and James Belushi; and Bongos, a Cuban-flavored cafe created by Gloria Estefan and her husband, Emilio. The Wide World of Sports complex has a branch of the Official All-Star Cafe chain, whose owner roster includes Andre Agassi, Monica Seles, Wayne Gretzky, Ken Griffey, Jr., and Shaquille O'Neal—who, it should be remembered in this promo-happy World, starred as the genial genie in Disney's *Kazaam!*

Not only film and sports stars, but Food Channel and food-magazine stars have been enlisted in the Disney World parade. Paul Bocuse was one of the eponymous Chefs de France who designed the menu for that restaurant and the Bistro de Paris in Epcot (and now that the building actually has a kitchen rather than hauling in food from outside commissaries, it does them much more credit). California's Wolfgang Puck is so celebrity-kitchen conscious that the TV monitors at his cafe-plex in the West Side show not sports or movies but the cooks at work.

Celebrity status notwithstanding, neither Wolfgang Puck's Cafe nor the Estefans' Bongos have drawn much praise from diners. The House of Blues, surprisingly enough, has done much better with its New Orleans–style jambalayas and gospel brunch.

There are not one but two super-trendy Rainforest Cafe branches, one at the renovated Disney Village Marketplace and a super-theatrical version at the entrance to Animal Kingdom, where the decor and Audio-Animatronic elephants make it fit right into the scenery there. Not surprisingly in a place where the sky "rains" and the stars flicker over head, more thought went into naming the dishes than perfecting the recipes.

In fact, although the "official" guides to Walt Disney World describe various restaurants as "delicious," "delectable," or "delightful"— George Gershwin, call your agent—the truth is that little of the food is first-rate. And the most disappointing restaurants in general are the often attractive but commissary-bland ethnic kitchens.

Most of the "ethnic" food is Americanized, or rather homogenized, especially at Epcot, where visitors from so many countries as well as the United States tend to have preconceived notions of egg rolls and enchiladas. The Teppanyaki Dining Room in the

Japan Pavilion happens to be one of the better restaurants in the World, with pretty good teppanyaki (and good tempura next door)—but it specializes in a particularly Westernized form of Japanese cuisine, first produced in New York only about 30 years ago. Ditto for Kimonos in the Swan; the food—some mainstream sushi, some tempura, some grilled skewers—is fair, but irregular. The Nine Dragons restaurant in the China Pavilion is nearly notorious for its cornstarch-heavy sauces; the egg roll cart at Adventureland is no worse. In fact, while the Asian-cuisine market is booming all over America, Disney World is having unusual trouble going along. Sum Chows, its super-trendy pan-Asian place in the Dolphin, has closed, and Kimonos seems in danger of becoming less rather than more authentic—less *kani* and more karaoke.

The buffet at Norway's Akershus isn't bad, but it's stodgy, smoky, and cheese- and mayonnaise-heavy. (Frankly, if smoked meats are your thing, the smoked turkey legs from the carts, which are enough for at least two people and only $4, are far better.) The exceptions are the San Angel Inn, a reasonably good Mexican (not Tex-Mex) restaurant beneath the "volcano" inside the Mexican pavilion; the surprisingly fun Marrakesh restaurant in the Moroccan pavilion; and the improved Chefs de France.

The only places the culinary staff actually recommend (off the record) are the classic-continental prix-fixe Victoria and Albert's at the Grand Floridian, where you pay $80 a head to have every waitress introduce herself as Vicky and all the waiters as Al; Seasons, the dining room at the Disney Institute, where if you're lucky the visiting "faculty" may have a couple of Michelin stars; and the modern-American California Grill, which has one of only seven ultra-chic Tom Shandley soufflé ovens in the United States. Arthur's 27 in the Wyndham Palace is the other super-fancy and super-pricey spot, like V&A's, more of a treat if you don't live in a good restaurant town, but not a thrill for New Yorkers.

The Chefs de France, as mentioned earlier, is now more of a credit to its executive chefs, Paul Bocuse, Gaston LeNotre, and Roger Verge; but it's still not much better than a B-plus. The two less formal restaurants in the Grand Floridian, the Mediterranean-style Citrico's and the modern-Floridian Narcossee's, are both making culinary gains. The various seafood specialists—the Cape May buffet in the Beach Club, Fulton's, the Flying Fish Cafe, and

Artist Point in the Wilderness Lodge—also have their adherents, especially among those who keep their eyes on nutritional advice.

Which is another thing: A lot of the food at Disney World, particularly the fast food, is not what you'd describe as healthy. (Funnel cakes? Happy meals?) This is one area that the parks have really attempted to address, and now there are fruit stands and juice bars scattered around, veggie sandwiches and chili, soft pretzels as well as the deceptively simple popcorn, baked potatoes (not, frankly, prepared with the apparent care of the turkey legs, but about one-tenth the calories and salt) as well as turkey leg carts, the frozen fruit bars in the ice cream freezers, and frozen yogurt or smoothies at the ice cream shops. Yes, it's hard, especially with all those fudge and cookie stands blasting chocolate at you, but stick to your guns. Look for the fruit markets in Liberty Square and Mickey's Toontown Fair in the Magic Kingdom, on Sunset Boulevard in the MGM Studios, and in the Harambe marketplace at Animal Kingdom.

And yes, okay, we will tell you the one junk food to blow your calorie budget on: As you cross the bridge between Future World and the World Showcase in Epcot, there's a little wagon just to the right, toward Canada, that sells cones of glazed pecans. Don't say we never spoiled you.

Picky Eaters

As a guest in "the World" you don't need to worry if you have special dietary needs. With the expansion of Disney's audience, not only to older visitors but also to those from other countries, the corporation has greatly increased its attention to special-requirement menus. With 24-hours' advance notice, you can have low-sodium, lactose-free, kosher, vegetarian, or vegan meals at most of the sit-down restaurants. There are even rumors that the restaurant in the planned Animal Kingdom Lodge—the hotel where every room will have a view of the live animals—will be entirely vegetarian, which seems only fair.

Part Nine

"Hidden Mickeys" and Other Grown-Up Games

As we pointed out in the Introduction, one thing Walt Disney and his army of Imagineers had in abundance was a shared sense of playfulness. They didn't think play was something that should be reserved for the under-age-12 crowd. There are literary, musical, and historical jokes all over the theme parks, in the hotels, and in rides. Even names—like the Merchant of Venus shop; or Pleasure Island, where people are in danger of making asses of themselves (which is what happens to the boys in *Pinocchio*). Only the most prodigious teenager is going to get even half the jokes in Robin Williams's rapid-fire riffs in *The Timekeeper*, among them such sophisticated puns as "doubting automaton," "chardonnay, gone tomorrow," and "all feet are the same," as in "auf wiedersein," the German phrase for farewell.

The Imagineers drew themselves and their colleagues into murals and caricatures, from Cinderella Castle to *The Hall of Presidents*. Their names and faces appear, in various disguises, in the tombstones of The Haunted Mansion, the singing busts, and ghostly apparitions. The name of the supposed owner of the mansion itself, Master Gracey, salutes Imagineer Yale Gracey. There are "credits" in the form of addresses on shipping crates at the Jungle Cruise and "memos" stuck on bulletin boards, like the one in Carousel of Progress that says, "Marty called—wants changes," referring to chief Imagineer Marty Sklar.

Friends of Walt, both high and low, make cameo appearances. In the scene in Pirates of the Caribbean in which a man in jail is trying to sneak the keys away, the man next to the dog is Sid Caesar; the white-haired prisoner is believed to have been modeled on a longtime janitor who often supplied Imagineers with ideas.

But far and away the single largest "game" in Disney World involves what are called "Hidden Mickeys," the pursuit of which has become more than a cult diversion and spawned dozens on Web sites and clubs. Hidden Mickeys are versions of that most recognizable silhouette used in places and ways that make them nearly unrecognizable. They may show up in maps, on rides, in the sky, on the ground, in vegetation, in furnishings, in hieroglyphics, and even in food (though those, as we'll explain in the moment, are usually "decor Mickeys," not hidden ones). They appear in clothes, on clock faces, in murals, in maps, and on mountains; they show up in wrought iron and wood, formed of lights, and made of shadow. They may be tiny or quite large—architectural in some cases—always visible, visible only from certain angles, permanently affixed, or flashing by in a video moment.

Most are the sort of face-forward outline often used to frame the credits of Mickey Mouse cartoons: a black circle with two smaller circles on top. Some are profiles, with a fourth and even smaller circle for the "nose" on one side, but always with the ears still in full frontal position. A few are ears mounted on a half-circle, representing the kind of mouse ear hats that fans can wear; and more rarely you'll find Mickeys with pointed hats, à la "The Sorcerer's Apprentice." Watch, too, for Mickey toys, souvenir mugs, and the like used as props within scenes. The last subcategory of Hidden Mickeys are his name, but not where you would expect it—on the sheet music in the library of The Twilight Zone Tower of Terror, for example, or (visible only to employees) inscribed along with Walt's in the manuscript of the sleeping monk in Spaceship Earth.

There are thousands of Mickeys—actually, millions, counting the wallpaper and carpeting—at least one in every ride and resort in the entire Disney World complex. There are so many in the Wilderness Lodge, in fact, that the cast members in the hotel sometimes organize scavenger hunts. So if you see people riding the same rides over and over and peering intently at something that seems perfectly ordinary to you, they are probably on the Mickey trail.

Hidden Mickeys, as we said, are integrated into their surroundings in a way that you might just walk right by them. Decor

Mickeys are more obvious, designed to add to your fun, but not disguised: The Mickey ears on the "Earful Tower," the water tower at MGM Studios, are decor Mickeys, for example; so are the three-lobed pats of butter and pancakes various restaurants produce and the Mickey design on the toilet paper in some of the resorts. But the ones woven into the overhead tapestries of the Polynesian Resort would count as hidden.

Some are virtual Mickeys, like the ones in DisneyQuest's Virtual Jungle Cruise, where the balloons that float through the sky sometimes (but not always) have ears; the ice arch always does, and so does the figure in the "Arabic" writing of the DisneyQuest carpeting.

There are Mickey tiles on the wood-burning oven at Wolfgang Puck's Express, punched into the tin roof of the House of Blues merchandise shop (just one—the rest are in line), and in the floor tiles near the entrance doors of the rest rooms at Cirque du Soleil.

Here is an extremely abbreviated list, just enough to give you an idea how extensive and how incredibly varied the hordes of Hidden Mickeys are. As a general hint, take a second look at any grouping of round items—skillets, pulleys, plates, wheels, gears, barrels, hubcaps, tires, rolled-up maps or blueprints, water lily pads, light bulbs, thumbtacks, clouds, flowers and flower pots, and so on. And we've listed a few more in "Part Six: Nightlife." Good hunting!

Hidden Mickeys in the Magic Kingdom

In Walt Disney World, of course, Mickey is a star. Sometimes he's even a constellation. In Space Mountain, for example, every third window has a constellation that looks oddly familiar; though it's not from any star map you've seen before, it is very like a constellation that shows up in a map on the wall of the Star Traders shop over at the Disney-MGM Studios, in the Disney Outfitters in Animal Kingdom, and again in The Twilight Zone Tower of Terror. Also in Space Mountain, during the video "news" montage that keeps visitors in the queue entertained, a suspiciously shaped satellite roars by.

In the mosaics along the walkway of the Cinderella Castle, King Stefan is caught browsing through a magazine with Mickey on the cover.

The Carousel of Progress, which was one of Walt's own creations (and which remains almost unchanged in his honor), is filled with Hidden Mickeys: from the trio of potted sunflowers in the "grandpa" segment to the shadows in the ironing pantry (when the grandmother nods her head) to the computer's screen saver in the Christmas scene. In fact, as the computer game shuts down, the last ship leaving the abandoned "planet" on the screen has a Mickey painted on the side. Compared to that, spotting the Mickey gifts they're exchanging and the wrapping paper they're in is easy.

In *Alien Encounter*, Mickey becomes an intergalactically recognizable hieroglyph (the sixth figure down in each set down the columns outside the entrance). In Timekeeper, when the 9-Eye character returns to modern-day Paris, there's a little girl holding the sort of silver Mickey-shaped balloons sold all over Disney World. And if you can't spot the three-lobed planet at least once in Buzz Lightyear's Space Ranger Spin, you need Mickey glasses.

In Frontierland, there's a three-lobed cactus in the shooting gallery; in Adventureland, several of the birds in the Tiki Room are sitting on Mickey-shaped perches and the trim over the Traders of Timbuktu shop goes round and round. The biggest draw here is the Jungle Cruise, of course, and there are plenty of Mickeys around there, starting with the one formed by the spare tire and bulging headlamps of the truck parked at the entrance. There are three-lobed chips out of the stone in the tunnel just before the elephant wading pool, in the Cambodian ruins, on the back of the spider guarding the treasure and as the three gold plates on the right under the snakes.

If you're really having trouble getting the concept here, go to Mickey's Toontown Fair to Mickey's Country House and check out the doors and the mirrors and the vegetables in Mickey's garden. Then look at the fencepost. Then—oh, never mind.

Hidden Mickeys in Epcot

On land, in the sea, in the sky, and beyond—and underfoot. Look at the carpet pattern at *Honey, I Shrunk the Audience.* The antenna near the racing dolphins in the underwater window outside Horizons, and the bubbles in the undersea home inside. The previously uncharted island off the east coast of Australia in Imagination Pavillion. And on the stars of Spaceship Earth.

In The Land pavilion, during the Living with the Land ride, the woman testing the water quality in the Willamette River is wearing sunglasses, in which are reflected a cameraman wearing a Mickey T-shirt. The farmer driving a harvester in *The Circle of Life* has a Mickey on his baseball cap, and the Native American on horseback is standing near a set of three stones.

Blood veins in the sign over the entrance to Body Wars form a Mickey; and although it's Epcot by proxy, if you look at the Body Wars posters behind the ticket booths at the Transportation and Ticket Center, you'll see three blood cells huddled together in just the right way.

Mickey makes it into several of the international pavilions of the World Showcase, too: as clay pots in the marketplace scene of Mexico's El Río del Tiempo ride, in Norway's Maelstrom ride (notice something weird about that Viking's "horns"?), in the clouds of a dragon mural in China; and in a second-story window in the wedding party scene in the *Impressions de France* film. He even has his place in American history; look at the wagon train painting in the lobby of *The American Adventure,* just above the first ox team.

Hidden Mickeys in MGM Studios

At the Disney-MGM Studios, the entire central plaza is a Mickey, but you almost have to be flying overhead to see it: The Brown Derby Restaurant and Echo Lake are the ears, and the big curved entrance to Graumann's Chinese Theatre is his smile. (We say *almost:* The easy way is to look at the map of the park.) In fact, at one stage or another, nearly all the theme parks have had familiar profiles, though additions and improvements have gradually fudged them.

In the waiting foyer of Mama Melrose's Ristorante Italiano, one of the Dalmatians has a three-lobed spot; check out the welding torch's three gauges in the ordering area of Rosie's Red Hot Dogs. The Mickeys are even odder (appropriately) at the Sci-Fi Dine-In Theater restaurant, including one in the branches of the tree to the left and behind the screen over the kitchen.

The Great Movie Ride, inside Mann's, has several, including Pharaoh Mickey (and cupbearer Donald) in the hieroglyphs of *Raiders of the Lost Ark* and a couple in Gangster Alley, one in the window over the bank that gets robbed and one on the billboard. In *Jim Henson's MuppetVision 4D,* the test pattern during Scooter's second crossover is a Mickey; there's one on the "Top 5 Reasons for Returning Your 3D Glasses" sign; and the balloons in the last scene are Mickey-fied.

At Christmas, when the New York block becomes the passage to the Osborne Brothers' holiday lights extravaganza, there are extra Mickeys added to the already blinding display: In fact, there are rumored to be as many as 100 of them. The third puff of smoke from the train, the face of one of the toy soldiers, and some of the windows in the house are Mickeys. The back of the clock tower has ears instead of the real clock face the other three sides have; and of course anywhere there are streetlights or glass balls, there are apt to be three clustered together.

Hidden Mickeys in the Animal Kingdom

Because it's fairly new, the Mickeys in this park are still being uncovered; but there are said to be more than a hundred in the mural above the Observation Station, worked into the pupils of eyes, markings on the back of insects, and so on. (There are also some on the shells of the animated insects in *It's Tough to Be a Bug!)* According to cast members, there are five Mickeys among the 360 animals mazed into the Tree of Life, one in the suction cups of the octopus's tentacles and another made of moss that the roadrunner's tail points to. There are also three smaller trees whose crowns overlap below the Tree of Life as you enter.

There is a Mickey in the knobs of one of the largest baobab trees in the Kilimanjaro Safari and also in the rocks on the right-hand side of the lions' den. Check out the water jug in the rafters of the Safari queue, too. There are some puddles in flamingo-land that set off a little island; a three-lobed manhole in the Harambe Marketplace (on the right just after you cross the bridge from Safari Village and pause in front of Tamu Tamu), and a quite large, pale Mickey in the concrete floor of the Harambe Fruit Market near the Pagnani Forest. Once you enter the Pagnani and walk into the hut that houses the naked mole-rat exhibit, there are several, one on the label of the aspirin bottle; the map near the suspension bridge at the gorilla habitat has one, too.

Just outside the women's rest room beyond the Pizzafari is a frog with some very spherical dots carved into its side. Even more elaborate is the mural inside the Pizzafari that proves the leopard can, indeed, change his spots—at least in Disney World. Nearby is a fire hydrant with an unusual nuts-and-bolts arrangement.

Just over the bridge into Asia is a cart loaded with logs, one of which has three holes drilled or rotted into it. There are stones in the path of the Maharaja Jungle Trek, and three swirls in the water of the river mural near the tiger viewing windows. There are others in the mural of the four kings, one a royal earring. And in the part of Mammoth Dig where children can unearth fossils, there is a Mickey constructed of a circular fan and two hard-hats hung on the wall.

And among the Hidden Mickeys in the Party O' Saurus sculpture outside Chester and Hester's is one of the double-joke sorts: a one-year cast member pin in the shape of Steamboat Willie, just to the upper right side of the silver pendant on his neck.

STAR-MAKER MACHINERY

There is a sort of specialized Hidden Mickey game that involves the films of Steven Spielberg and George Lucas, both of whom grew up Walt Disney fans. (Remember that "When You Wish Upon a Star" is the climactic music of *Close Encounters of the Third Kind;* Lucas produced one of Disney World's first super video-era attractions, Michael Jackson's *Captain Eo.*) Some are tributes, and some are brainteasers aimed at serious movie buffs.

For instance, when the rear half of the plane that was used in *Casablanca* was bought and moved to the *Indiana Jones Epic Stunt Spectacular* at Disney-MGM Studios, Imagineers drilled and reshaped three holes in the metal to get a Mickey into the mix. (Talk about movie pedigrees! The whole airplane should probably be bronzed.)

As mentioned, Mickey and Donald are in the hieroglyphs of the *Raiders of the Lost Ark* segment of the Great Movie Ride, as are robots C3PO and R2D2. There are several Hidden Mickeys in Lucas's Star Tours: One of the baby Ewoks is carrying a stuffed Mickey toy, and the first G2 robot is wearing a Mickey Mouse watch. There's also one on the "phone directory" sign in the waiting queue.

Lucas himself returns the favor by making a couple of guest appearances: Visitors waiting to enter Star Tours hear a call for "Egroeg Sacul," which is George Lucas spelled backward. A hazardous materials truck has a registration number that is (or at least was) the phone number for Lucasfilms and license plate number THX 1138, the name of an early Lucas film. These are the Hidden Georges. He makes an intentional appearance during the Disney-MGM Studios Tour as well.

There are a few give-and-take salutes to other Disney collaborators. One great sight gag is at Pleasure Island, where the rotating giant dinosaur next to Planet Hollywood in Pleasure Island is a dead ringer for Earl Sinclair, the Jackie Gleason–like *pater tyrannosaurus* of the cult classic TV satire "Dinosaurs"; a Jim Henson production, the series cheerfully lampooned not only politics and modern culture but also television and movies themselves.

HIDDEN FLICKIES

There is one other type of hidden tribute woven throughout the park: what might be called "hidden flickies," or movie and TV clips slipped without fanfare into other sets in addition to the intentional clips. Many are Disney's own: The Little Mermaid is among the items dumped into the "brain" at Cranial Command; a hidden Pocahontas has been spotted in the newsreel at Space Mountain; in *The Making of Me,* the parents go in to see *20,000 Leagues Under the Sea,* which also appears in Spaceship Earth; the preshow of *Alien Encounter* has film from *Mission to Mars,* the show that the *Encounter* replaced; and bits from *The Black Hole* are visible at Dreamfinder's home. And music at The Twilight Zone Tower of Terror, in addition to the familiar da-DA-da-da, includes the ghostly theme from *The Shining*—which is a tip of the hat to the Stephen King–like plot. Heeeeeere's Mickey!

The most concentrated group of tributes, in fact, is built into The Twilight Zone Tower of Terror and are, not surprisingly, to the Rod Serling TV series itself. Imagineers viewed every one of the 156 original episodes at least twice and most of Serling's introductions more often than that, before piecing together the video. And *Twilight Zone* memorabilia is displayed throughout the ride—enough to spark a new Hidden Serling chase among his fans. Some of the props displayed in the building are the broken glasses from "Time Enough at Last," the heartbreaking story in which book lover Burgess Meredith survives a nuclear holocaust only to drop and break his only pair of eyeglasses; the alien "cookbook" from "To Serve Man"; and a miniature robot invader.

Although it's not visible at Disney World (but we assume you're hooked now), there is another sort of Hidden Mickey evolving, and those are images animators sneak into films so quickly that they can barely been seen. (Actually, they've been doing it for decades, but with the advent of videos, which can slow down the action, some of the more risqué inserts have been spotted and withdrawn.) Early in *The Little Mermaid,* for example, Mickey, Goofy, and Donald make a don't-blink appearance in the parade crowd. In *Aladdin,* as the magically transformed Rajah begins to turn back from a cub into a tiger, he briefly morphs into Mickey. Similarly, in *The Lion King,* when the monkeys haul Zazu up into the tree, they pull a yellow Mickey out of his head—but faster than the naked eye can see without the slow motion control.

In *Who Framed Roger Rabbit?* there is bathroom graffiti that reads, "For a good time, call Allyson Wonderland." (Not only that, but until the video police got it, one frame had Michael Eisner's phone number underneath.) In one of the *Roger Rabbit* sequels, *Tummy Trouble,* there's a curtain in the hospital over which is draped a pair of red shorts and under which is a pair of yellow shoes. In another Roger short, *Roller Coaster Rabbit,* stuffed Mickeys are the prizes at a darts booth, and Mickey ears are among the "ballast" tossed out of the car.

It's not just Mickey and friends, either. *Aladdin,* in fact, is full of cameo appearances—Pinocchio, Sebastian the Crab, a Beast toy, and a whole raft of caricatured Imagineers and animators are visible. Belle walks through the Paris of *The Hunchback of Notre Dame* reading a book just as she does in her own village; and Pumbaa the warthog of *The Lion King* is hanging from a pole.

PUN-ISHING TREATMENT

Whenever you pass a sign on a shop or read a caption of some sort, think twice: How about the M. T. Lott Real Estate Investments company along the Magic Kingdom's Main Street? Or Safen Sound, the home port of the now-stranded shrimp boat Miss Tilly atop Typhoon Lagoon?

Some are really inside jokes; near the M. T. Lott sign is the Pseudonym Real Estate Development Co., which refers back to when Disney's lieutenants set up layers of dummy corporations to buy Orlando property without setting off a land rush. The names on the sign are Bob Foster, one of the attorneys who set up those post office box "corporations," and Bill Davis, the pseudonym used by Walt Disney himself.

In DinoLand U.S.A., as you wander through the skeleton display on the way to Countdown to Extinction, you'll hear such pop songs as "I Fall to Pieces" and "It's the End of the World as We Know It." As you pass the Jungle Cruise, you may hear, but not focus on, Cole Porter's catchy "You're the Top," which includes the lyrics, "You're the melody from a symphony by Strauss/You're an O'Neill drama/You're Whistler's Mama—You're Mickey Mouse!"

Some of the jokes around Disney World are so in that they require an explanation—or a PhD. The Greek being quoted by the actors in Spaceship Earth is from Sophocles's *Oedipus Rex,* and according to the Disney-authorized guide by Jeff Birnbaum, the type on Gutenberg's press is actually movable (and the page he is proofing is copied from the Huntington Library's Gutenberg Bible). Some in-jokes are almost like philosophical debates: The skeletons that are playing chess in the Pirates of the Caribbean ride are actually at stalemate (would that make it a dead draw?).

And as Disney World becomes more seriously interested in the Third World (as opposed to the Small World), via Animal Kingdom's quite authentic Asian and African sections, the Imagineers are beginning to bring in equally "classical" references from other cultures, like the illustrations inside the pavilion in Kali River Rapids, which are from the *Jakata Tales,* a sort of *Aesop's Fables* of India. And jokes, of course: Ask the cast members around the Wildlife Express station to translate some of the signs.

Part Ten

Shopping in Walt Disney World

Hanging around in Walt Disney World eventually reminds you of that old line: Money can't buy you love . . . but it helps.

A true Disney World devotee would undoubtedly say that money is no object, and maybe it's not—but there are certainly a lot of *objets* that require it. Considering that in one store or another in Walt Disney World, you can find (in addition to the obvious T-shirts, Pooh sunglasses, and such): furniture, fanny packs, rugs, artwork, accessories, autographs, antiques and collectibles, underwear and unmentionables, linens, perfumes, soaps, cookware, chopsticks, crystal, chess sets, Beatles dolls, Barbie dolls, balloon chairs, bean bag chairs, bonsai, bug eyes, Mickey ears, musical instruments, musical recordings, wildlife recordings, puppets, LEGO kits, vintage bikes, bottles, pottery, leather, chocolate truffles, coffee mugs, calculators, candles, clocks, rubber masks, radios, sunglasses, spices, socks, swords, telephones, topiaries, videos, picture frames, watches, designer wear, and China doll pajamas—and on and on—and you can expect the price tags to work their way up.

On the other hand, as you can also see, there are plenty of clever, attractive, and even durable souvenirs you can find without breaking either your back or your budget. Or your blisters. We've done the advance work for you, so even if you're only going to a single park, you can probably find something you like. If you get tired, there's probably something you can pick up at your hotel. In fact, we've done all the work—just skip right down to our list

139

of "The Best Souvenirs in the World," and you won't even have to look around. And if worse comes to absolute worst, there's a Disney merchandise store in the Orlando airport.

That's the first cautionary note: There's Disney stuff *everywhere*. You can't walk ten feet without tripping over a kiosk, boutique, vendor, or attraction shop. Make sure whatever you buy is really something you want, because chances are you'll see something else you like in five minutes.

Second, a huge amount of this stuff is repetitious. With the exception of Epcot's World Showcase shops, the vast preponderance of merchandise in Disney World is either marked with a Disney logo, movie, character, or slogan of some sort. These characters migrate from park to park, so to speak, so that you can find Buzz Lightyear or the *Bug's Life* greenie almost anywhere. (Which is another reason to be deliberate in your purchasing; you'll probably have another opportunity to get whatever it is if you don't find something better.)

Prices are pretty uniform, just for this reason; so if you seem to see the same shirts with different price tags, check the labels; most T-shirts sold in Disney World are 100% cotton, but some may be a lighter weight.

Finally, there's one sort of "merchandising" we're not crazy about. Call them stealth souvenirs. Or in some cases, stalking and selling. This has to do with cast members, often in sort of period dress with a press card in the hat band and so on, who pop up and offer to take your instant color or digital photograph. (Actually, though most are clearly identifiable as cast members, some might initially be mistaken for fellow tourists.) They are frequently hanging around where the big architectural features such as Spaceship Earth or Cinderella Castle make for dramatic and instantly recognizable backgrounds. You might be invited to try it out for free: See the picture, and if you don't like it, you don't have to buy it—classic pressure stuff. (And a few minute later, you'll find that you could have sent a free email postcard of yourself, with the big geodesic Earth seemingly right behind your head, from a booth inside Innoventions.)

Here's another twist on the same spiel: Several of the thrill rides have digital cameras in them at certain spots, so that when you come out, you are offered a copy of a photo in which your entire boat/space transport/elevator car is seen looking terrified, screaming, clutching, laughing, and so on. With the adrenaline still racing, it seems like a fun idea. But a copy of the photo, in a cardboard folder or sometimes in a more expensive and only slightly less tacky frame, can cost $10 or $12. Some older visitors in particular feel a little guilty about not buying these Polaroids or group photos, but you should feel absolutely no pressure to do so. We can tell you from experience that most of these shots, although fun at the time, quickly lose their appeal.

If you want photographs of yourself at Disney World, it's more fun to get one of those cheap single-use cameras, which are quite good outside, and take them yourself. Better yet, take photos of one another with the live characters who wander everywhere; they are perfectly happy to pose with grown-ups. It's their job. In fact, anecdotal evidence suggests that in Epcot's World Showcase, at least, there are more adults, and foreign tourists especially, who pose with either characters or international entertainers than children. It seems rather odd that there are also places within Disney World where you can have your photograph artificially and expensively merged with cardboard characters or backgrounds, but some visitors get caught up in the fun and don't think. (That's why you have this book, right?)

With rare exceptions, we have not evaluated the merchandise available at the various restaurants, particularly those that are branches of national chains: A Planet Hollywood T-shirt is a Planet Hollywood T-shirt, wherever you get it; if you are determined to have one from every city you can, you'll be standing in line to buy it with or without our urging. However, we would like to tip our ears to the folks at the House of Blues paraphernalia shop at Disney's West Side, because at least one set of leather jackets there has absolutely no advertising on it. No logo, no name, no nothing. Thanks, guys.

Similarly, we haven't focused on the hotel shops and concourses (we'll just mention two as stand-outs, Dabblers in the Disney Institute and the hotel boutique at Wilderness Lodge). If you understand that most of the resort shops go with the resort theme, you'll have a pretty good idea what you can find. So if you're just desperate for beignet mix, go over to Port Orleans. But if you have an idea of what you want, but aren't sure where it might be, shop "on line," so to speak, by calling the merchandise experts at (407) 824-5566 and asking them if and where it's available. (And of course, you really can shop online when you get home, if you have second thoughts about that Mickey Mouse watch.)

Finally, if you are one of those people who cannot take a vacation without getting outlet-mall fever, Orlando's two main choices are **Belz Factory Outlet World** (phone (407) 354-0126), at the north end of International Drive, with 180 name-brand shops such as Dansk, Reebok, Timberland, Bruno Magli, and Osh Kosh B'Gosh (bargain hunters should certainly check out the discontinued and therefore discounted but otherwise undetectable Disney merchandise at the Character Warehouse); and the adjoining **International Designer Outlets** (phone (407) 354-0300), which has Saks Off Fifth, Coach, Ann Taylor, Donna Karan, and so on.

Pack Rats

Remember that if you are staying at one of the Walt Disney World resorts, you can have your merchandise or souvenirs delivered to the hotel or at least taken up to the park entrance so you can pick it up at your convenience. You may not think that zebra-striped candle is much to carry, but believe me, in about 30 minutes, you'll be tempted to lose it. Or it will be covered in barbecue sauce. And since, as you will be frequently reminded, FedEx is the official shipper of Disney World, you can send larger or fragile items directly to your home.

Downtown Disney

DISNEY VILLAGE MARKETPLACE

Shopping has probably long since replaced baseball as America's national pastime; but only the Walt Disney Company could figure out a way to make it into a whole theme park.

Disney Village Marketplace, which underwent a very expensive renovation a couple of years ago in which, among other things, the old Chef Mickey's was transformed into a Rainforest Cafe, is the single most complete souvenir shop in Disney World. It's also the longest-running attraction in Disney World, in terms of daily access: The shops there open at 9:30 a.m. every morning and stay open until 11 p.m. at night, 11:30 on weekends.

The Marketplace serves not only as a commodities market but also as an intentionally enticing gateway to Pleasure Island and Disney's West Side; all three areas are referred to together as Downtown Disney, and none of them requires an admission ticket during the day. Only Pleasure Island requires a ticket after 7 p.m. The Marketplace restaurants, like those in the West Side, are basically chain operations, designed to draw in some local lunch trade, and also stay open until 11 p.m.; if you are staying at one of the resorts that use Downtown Disney as a bus transfer spot, such as Dixie Landings and Port Orleans, they may offer you a way of grabbing an easy carry-home dinner.

The parking lot at Downtown Disney stays open until 2 a.m., because of the nightclubs at Pleasure Island and Disney's West Side. There is valet parking, which costs $5—free to handicapped visitors—which may seem expensive, but if you are one of those people who loses cars in parking lots, it may be worthwhile: The lots stretch alongside all three sections, looking rather alot alike, and, after dark especially, you may have trouble rediscovering the spot. In fact, it happens all the time.

There are a few stores here that stock merchandise for the homeowner who doesn't necessarily want to endorse the Disney company in every room of the house, but most of the shops are Disney-oriented in a really big way—particularly the 12-room **World of Disney**. This is almost a compendium of every sort of character merchandise Disney makes, covering more than 50,000 square feet: furniture, toys, baby bunting, character candy, T-shirts, books, videos, and so on. If you are shopping for Disney-approved merchandise, you can probably get your entire list of gifts here. But since it is a shopping showplace, the smaller stores of the Marketplace do have some more interesting ideas, several of which make it into our list of Disney World's best souvenirs below. In general, follow our leads:

For business travelers or those who unexpectedly find themselves in need of something at least a little nicer than Bermuda shorts, the Marketplace has two clothing stores offering what would be perfectly respectable, though unremarkable, replacements for damaged conference or dinner attire. **Resortwear Unlimited** has informal day and evening clothes for women, along with Lancôme cosmetics in case you're on your way to a last-minute party; the outfits aren't cheap, but they're not much more expensive than you'd find at any resort.

The men's shop is called **Harrington Bay Clothiers,** and the staff there has a pretty relaxed attitude toward their position in the Marketplace. "Wow, nothing with names on it!" one browser exclaimed with relief. "Well, yes and no," smiled the clerk. "At least there's no Mickey. It's all Ralph, Calvin, or Tommy"—meaning Lauren, Klein, and Hilfiger, respectively. And he was right.

There's plenty of Mickey at **Team Mickey's Athletic Club,** on the other hand, but usually combined with the ubiquitous Nike swoosh and other logos. It's pretty predictable stuff, although you can get a quick score update from the ESPN monitors; but unless you really want to lift weights with a newly buff Tigger on your thong leotard (another "cute" idea that quickly wears thin) or show up at the country club with Pooh "booties" on your golf club, your local athletic wear discounter is a better deal.

The **Gourmet Pantry** isn't overwhelming in its supply of edibles, but if you do want to make your own picnic basket, it's probably one of your few choices. More intriguingly, it has a number of the newly trendy kitchen appliances designed by Michael Graves (of the Dolphin and Swan resorts) including the little pocket accessories you may have forgotten, such as wine openers and stoppers. They also offer some of the funnier and less expensive Disney gifts, along the lines of a Mickey and Minnie bridal couple salt and pepper set, which might be a great gag wedding shower present.

The **2R's,** or Reading & Riting, store has a broad assortment of Disney-associated books (Milne's Pooh stories, for example), videos, notepaper and cards, pencils, stamps, and so on. It even has some Mickey phones and magnet photo frames. Its most interesting offerings, however, are a small collection of modern office accessories; see "The Best Souvenirs in 'the World'" below.

2R's opens into the **Art of Disney,** one the three or four stores around Disney World where animation cels from Disney films—really authorized reproductions, note—and cartoon figurines are sold. This store wins a star for its Mickey chair (see "The Best Souvenirs in 'the World,'" below), and for some of the reconceived "portraits" of Mickey by modern artists; but it also goes overboard with some rather tacky offerings as well. We're thinking specifically of a pair of crystal wedding flutes with Mickey and Minnie grinning happily, which somehow seems like a less great shower gag, especially at $95 a set.

Disney's Days of Christmas is just what it sounds like. Personally, we think year-round Christmas stores should be abolished because it takes all the fun out of the holidays, but considering that New Year's Eve is celebrated every night only a few hundred feet away on Pleasure Island, it's not a surprise that Disney would market its stocking cap ears, Christmas tree Tiggers, and Uncle Scrooges ("bah, honk!") 365 days a year. Nor is it a surprise to see Animal Kingdom Barbie and her other customized friends filling a store called **Toys Fantastic**, with the subtitle, "Presented by Mattel." Don't worry about skipping this shop, either; Barbie, Buzz and all their friends are everywhere in the theme parks.

A much more honestly delightful toy shop is the **LEGO Imagination Center,** a superstore of LEGO toys with fantastic whole movie sets revolving in window cases, some of which look almost like spoofs of Disney sets elsewhere. There's an underwater city that evokes the one in Spaceship Earth and hidden temples that suggest a cross between the Indiana Jones stunt show and *Fantasmic!* You can spend half an hour admiring these incredibly ornate and witty constructions—and you really should; if they were for sale they would sweep the "best souvenirs" awards—and another little while in the playground, where there are tables and stacks of LEGO pieces for kids and less self-conscious adults to play with. If you need inspiration, check out the "Loch Ness monster" over the side and the dinosaur garden around you. (LEGO adjoins the McDonald's, which is designed to look like Ronald McDonald's playhouse, and occasionally you see people, slightly befuddled, wandering around the more-than-life-sized creations in one building looking for the other.)

There's a garden-supply shop with small topiary frames shaped like Mickey and Donald and some bonsai specimens (neither of which, frankly, looked in terrific condition the last time we were there, and certainly not as good as the bonsai at the Japan pavilion in Epcot), an all-Pooh store and a Disney bean-bag and plush animal emporium that is nearly always crawling with children. There's also a photo store where you can have your picture morphed into a background with Mickey or Donald, and so on. But we've been through that.

More to the adult taste might be **Disney At Home,** which has bath and bedroom furnishings that would cheer up a guest room or kid's room or poolhouse. The most pretentious, or precious, depending on your outlook, store in the complex may be the **Eurospain** crystal store, which loads up a large room with those "Bohemian" wine goblets with different-colored bowls, beer steins, crystal mermaids, rainbow dangles, fairy castles, and so on — a lot of which is very like crystal sold in the various areas of the Epcot World Showcase. We say, if you're going to buy an expensive glass Eiffel Tower, at least do it in "France." But if you want a glass slipper, this is the spot.

Aside from the Rainforest Cafe (which has its own merchandise shop, of course) and the McDonald's, the Marketplace offers what's called Cap'n Jack's Oyster Bar (not a real raw bar), a Ghirardelli soda fountain and chocolate shop that smells like heaven, a non-alcoholic waterside bar called Sunset Cove, and a Wolfgang Puck Express, which offers nouveau–L.A. pizzas and pastas.

Incidentally, you can rent pontoons and canopy boats at the Marina, and maybe take your Pantry package out onto the water; but you have to have it back by 5 p.m., so lunch or cocktails only. Or you could arrange a "fishing trip," all equipment supplied, if you don't mind throwing back anything that you catch.

PLEASURE ISLAND AND DISNEY'S WEST SIDE

Pleasure Island has a sort of Jekyll and Hyde personality, part shopping strip, part nightclub cluster; although the Jekyll-boutique side is definitely the weaker of the two.

From 10:30 a.m. to 7 p.m., visitors may wander through Pleasure Island without paying for admission, but only a handful of stores and vendors (including a temporary tattoo parlor) are actually open during the day. One is another Disney art gallery rather wittily called **Suspended Animation,** with limited-edition reproductions of animation cels, figurines, movie posters, and so on; the slant is a little more to the dark side (villains instead of heroines) at **Music Legends.** There are non-Disney clothing stores here, but neither **Aviators Supply** (for adults) or **Changing Attitudes** (teens) stock anything you couldn't get in any suburban mall, or discount clothing mart, either. **Island Depot** is a

Pleasure Island logo store for those who do prefer their T-shirts to have commercial endorsements; the usual character merchandise is found at **DTV.**

There are a couple of more intriguing spots, however. **Super-star Studios** is like a permanent karaoke party; you can either just sing to a prerecorded and embellished soundtrack, and take the cassette home, or you can actually make a video, with back-drop and your companions doing the Motown clap beside you. Admittedly, this may be more to the 30- and 40-something golden oldie crowd, but there's nearly always a Sinatra fan in the bunch.

And **Reel Finds** resells celebrity memorabilia that is, or was, up-close and personal—namely, clothing. Cher's black toreador/tux dinner jacket was going for a mere $225; Elton John's black silk band-collar shirt for $275. Black marcasite and rhinestone earrings of the sort that are hot all over New York City are here at about the same price as the new ones, only $30, but with real romance attached; they were worn by an extra in the gloriously swoony Zefferelli film of *Romeo and Juliet.* And for the really dis-cerning, there's a black Chanel clutch that belonged to Claudette Colbert for only $50; don't ask us why it's still there.

The West Side is Disney's most direct attempt to appeal to the new upscale (or wannabe) gen-X and boomer-excess consumer. This is label-loyalty central. Not only are most of the restaurants here either franchises or name brands—Planet Hollywood, the House of Blues, the Wolfgang Puck Cafe, Gloria Estefan's Bongos Cafe, and Fulton's Crab House and the Portobello Yacht Club, both owned and operated by the fantastically successful Chicago-based Levy Restaurant group—but several of the stores are simi-larly celebrity-connected, such as the **Virgin Megastore** and **All-Star Gear,** a sort of off-premises merchandise shop for the All-Star Cafe line, fronted by athletes Andre Agassi, Shaquille O'Neal, Monica Seles, Wayne Gretzky, Ken Griffey, Jr., and Joe Montana. (Except for the photos, incidentally, this is an athletic-wear store like any other.)

The West Side is trying to be a little bit hipper than most of the rest of Disney World, too: It plays to the neo-mogul style with a cigar store, fashion wannabes with a designer glasses frames store, and what may be the first New Age–style furnishings and acces-sories shop in Disney World. (Walt wouldn't have got the New Age attitude at all; he preferred re-imagining to the universe to surrendering to it.) The Zen store is called **Hoypoloi** (which might seem slightly insulting to those who fancy themselves more highly evolved than the run-of-the-mill tourist), and offers miniature plug-in fountains and desk-top Zen gardens with pencil-sized rakes, incense, glass pens, candles, wall hangings, sake and tea sets, and other Asian-influenced dishes. Depending on where you live, it may or may not seem new and fresh to you.

On the other hand, unless you're living in an underdeveloped country, you might think it a waste of time to go music shopping at Walt Disney World—except that, typically, this is bigger than your average shopping-mall record store. A Birnbaum guide refers to the **Virgin Megastore** ungrammatically but rather revealingly as "an enormity." It's as much entertainment as sales room—there are more than 300 CD listening booths and 20 laserdisc previewing booths where you can watch video films, sort of like testing out your own future-mogul home entertainment center. It's open until 1 a.m. during the week and until 2 a.m. Fridays and Saturdays.

The **Sosa Family** cigar emporium sells hand-rolled cigars, which, if you remember that Florida is the next thing to Cuba itself, may be just the thing for stogie-loving cousins who swear that only Havanas are worth having. (Or maybe you shouldn't tell them.)

The two big-money shops at the West Side are **Guitar Gallery** and **Starabilia.** Guitar Gallery, which seems weirdly out of place, sells both new and classic antique acoustic and electric guitars; only the rare hyper-collector needs to have a guitar shipped home from Disney World, though if you've been looking for a Gibson Hummingbird for 20 years, you'll be ecstatic.

Starabilia is one of several elaborate celebrity-memorabilia shops around Disney World, and it takes its price tags seriously. It has vintage bicycles (a late 1940s Donald Duck Whizzer), old-fashioned Coke machines, Beatles dolls, old arcade games (Merlin the Magician picks your card and tells your fortune), and lots of famous musicians' guitars (see "The Best Souvenirs in 'the World,'" below). This is a great place to browse, but be sure you read those price tags carefully; that Whizzer bike is $7,995, with a period and two zeros after the 5.

Celebrity Eyeworks would like to be a memorabilia store, but the movie-star stuff is just backdrop for expensive eyeglass frames.

Unless you've managed to mangle your Armanis while in Disney World, you can probably do just as well back home. Similarly, unless you're a line-dance addict and there's no Western wear/dude shop anywhere near you, you might find some fringe to your liking at the **Wildhorse Store,** but it's not particularly unusual stuff. If you are the refrigerator magnet type, you can find anything you want at **Magnetron,** but you can also save yourself 20 mindless minutes if you pass it up.

One of the West Side's most prestigious "franchise" operations of all is the new permanent home of **Cirque de Soleil,** which glows at the far end of the West Side like the ultimate fairy tale castle. Its near-fanatic following are sure to hang out in its merchandise store, which includes everything from videos of past shows and CDs of soundtracks to clown hats, balancing toys, embroidered jeans jackets, ties with silk acrobats and so on. Even those who've never seen the show will probably be drawn to the building.

Theme Park Shopping

Let us be frank here: Disney World is the most successful ongoing commercial in the world. Got a bug cartoon in the theaters? Make some bug dolls. Got a safari ride? Get me Barbie's wardrobe people! Was *Mulan* a hit? Let's have a parade! That'll make those dragon T-shirts even more popular.

In other words, Disney is there precisely to sell you something. Actually, they're there to sell you everything—a fairy tale, a day in the park, an idealized history of America, a video, a camera, a watch, a warm-up jacket . . . you name it. In fact, they even sell themselves as products for other commercial sponsors: Ride Buzz Lightyear's Space Ranger Spin, "presented by Mattel." Or the Barnstormer at Goofy's Wiseacre Farm, "presented by Friskies." Stop in for souvenirs at the Yankee Trader, "presented by the J. M. Smucker Company." Even the trams down Main Street are "presented by National Car Rental."

So you can't get more than 20 feet without having the opportunity to purchase something. We're not about to try to describe every store, and in any case, about the thirtieth time we said such-and-such a vendor stall stocks Aladdin dolls or Pooh topiary, they would have updated their inventory. And fully three-quarters could fit the description "carries Disney clothing." So we're only going to mention a few of the more interesting stores along the way.

THE MAGIC KINGDOM

Can't wait to buy your first souvenir? In the Magic Kingdom, there's almost nothing but shopping all the way up Main Street, so from the minute you walk through the railroad station arches till you stand in the shadow of Cinderella Castle, you are fair game for shopkeepers. In fact, the game isn't always so fair. Smell that fudge? You should—the aroma is being shot at you by what employees have nicknamed "smellitzers," fragrance cannons. (This priority of merchandise over make-believe is pretty revealing; though as the theme parks evolved, the sales tactics grew a little more subtle.)

The clothing in the various shops is all character stuff; you only have to decide whether you want casual wear or sweatshirts. **Disney Clothiers** is fairly typical; it only gets a special nod because those black velvet vests with Mickey and Minnie in Christmas skating outfits were pretty cute. (Slightly more fashionable stuff, as character clothing goes, is at **Sir Mickey's** in Fantasyland.)

The **Main Street Gallery,** which is in the left-hand corner of the Main Street circle as you enter, is another of the several animation-cel boutiques, but it has a few other interesting offerings as well, such as a $995 Ralph Kent chess set pitting a four-inch white-hatted cowboy-king Mickey and queen Minnie against a relatively towering six-inch black-hatted Pluto and his feisty "queen" Donald. Or a more adorable, and more portable, crystal Dumbo for $175. And for the executive who has everything, check out the Mickey-ish Cross pens at Uptown Jewelers (see also the office stuff at Number 10 in the best souvenirs list, below).

Frankly, our favorite Main Street "souvenir" is even more portable than the pen, but unfortunately it isn't permanent: It's a haircut. The **barber shop** that is tucked around the corner in a sort of alley behind the flower stall is staffed by hair stylists who give men's cuts for a measly $12 and women's for only $15. Unfortunately, they are no longer allowed to give shaves.

Swashbucklers ought to make time to visit the **King's Gallery** at Cinderella Castle, where they can restock their own private palace with tapestries, swords, and so on. Hidden Mickey seekers should know that we recently spotted a great Space Mountain T-shirt in the **Merchant of Venus** (a shop we'd patronize just for the name) that placed a space-suited astronaut strategically in front of twin moons. There's another Christmas shop in Liberty Square, but you already know how we feel about that. Beaded belts and bolos are among the more intriguing and potentially useful items at the **Frontier Trading Post** in Frontierland; teenagers will probably find some beads or earrings at **House of Treasure** in Adventureland, but there is better stuff elsewhere.

EPCOT

Jules Verne didn't know the half of it. You can go around the world in about 80 ways at Epcot, both technologically (via the Internet, virtual reality, or plain old imagination) or by ranging through the international pavilions. Either way, there is a lot of good stuff to spend money on in this park; since it can easily take two days to experience, you'd better expect to succumb. But frankly, the better souvenir stuff is not in Future World, but in the World Showcase, the upper part of the barbell-shaped park. (Skim the best souvenirs list below, and you'll see why we like it.)

For instance, Innoventions is chock-full of games to play and inventions to eye, but the carry-out versions don't seem to stand out. (Can you really re-create a virtual-reality game in your garage?) Besides, quite a lot of it, such as the IBM Internet of the future stuff, is pure advertisement: See now, buy later. You can see now, buy now at the online shopping networks and catalogs, which seems really crass. Or, as in the case of a few computer games, get hooked and get a copy. There are gardening implements and cute aprons at The Land, and undoubtedly a Test Track helmet is in the works; but even if you think you've spotted something, wait until you pass back through on your way out, because the World Showcase—which is, if you hadn't realized it, as much shopping mall as travelogue—has a lot more to offer.

Moving counterclockwise around the lagoon, the first national pavilion you come to is **Canada,** which stocks some very nice Native American animal sculptures and jewelry; some heavy, lumberjack-style jackets and plaid shirts; soft, plushy oversweaters; and even a few jackets with fur trim. (There's a leather-working stall on the promenade out front, and if you have an exhibitionist friend, you could have "Boy Toy" embossed on a belt for him.)

Next is the **United Kingdom,** and though the shortbread and Earl Grey at the Tea Cozy is nice, it's not exactly rare. Some of the Royal Doulton at the Queen's Table is rare, but its price is even more rarefied. Better souvenir finds: clan tartan ties at Pringle of Scotland and some lovely and less familiar fairy-tale books at Magic of Wales.

From the United Kingdom you cross a small bridge over a very European-looking canal, one nearly as small as the English Channel, toward the Eiffel Tower and **France.** Here you can buy one of several wines by the glass, including Mumm's Cordon Rouge champagne, and then sit out in the sunshine on a bench right out of Paris—you can buy whole bottles as souvenirs, of course—and the perfumes (at La Signature) and Provençal-style pottery (La Maison du Vin) are always in style.

Next to France is another favorite, the **Morocco** pavilion, which has almost everything except the glove-flexible leather slippers the acrobats there wear. (We asked.) Here, almost everything is spectacular, and most everything is a bargain: embroidered tunic-and-trouser sets like those that Pier 1 Imports used to sell, in jewel-like colors for about $125 a suit; charmingly irregular glass bottles; hand-knotted rugs; mosaic and ceramic platters; and one-world-chic leather bags.

And just beyond Morocco—in this World, anyway—lies the pavilion of **Japan**, another shopping and cultural highlight. In fact, if you were pressed for time and could only visit a segment of the park, the trio of France, Morocco, and Japan would be your best choice. (Especially if you don't get there until late in the day, because Japan has a great view of the *IllumiNations* display.)

Japan is one of the most evocative and scenic of the World Showcase areas, because while the Leaning Tower of Pisa or the Eiffel Tower are instantly recognizable, they also have a certain kitsch value because of all the jokes and puns made on them. The architecture of Japan, on the other hand, we recognize only for its elegance and style (though the building references are equally famous to the Japanese, of course). The Mitsukoshi Department Store, for example, is modeled on the late-eight-century Gosho Imperial Palace in Kyoto; the lovely pagoda on the other side of the courtyard, where jugglers, puppet masters, storytellers, and kodo drummers provide free entertainment, is copied from an equally revered temple. This is a great place to stock up on sake and tea sets, origami kits, full-sized kimonos and doll-sized ones (on dolls, of course), "raw pearls" (see "The Best Souvenirs in 'the World'," below), bonsai plants, and the tiny carved pilgrims and animals called *netsuke.* It's also a personal favorite place to slip away in the late afternoon for a little sushi and sake, with a restorative view of the Japanese gardens or the lagoon.

Next to Japan and directly across from the entrance bridge—sitting on "top" of the World, so to speak—is the **American Adventure,** housed in a building that is supposed to combine various intrinsically familiar bits of colonial landmarks, but ends up looking rather more like one of those "family-style" all-you-can-stuff-down buffets. Unless you're here for the show, which you will probably have to see, grain of salt not withstanding (see our explanation in "Part Four: The Big Four"), you can skip this and visit your own Ben Franklin next Fourth of July.

Italy's pavilion is pretty laid-back compared to some, and a lovely place to sit for a while in the sculpture garden, but it's not a shopper's paradise; the two best bets around here are the Venetian glass (not cheap—is any crystal in Disney World a bargain?) and, depending on where you live, the foodstuffs and Italian wines (not super-fine, but convenient).

Germany's main attractions are wines (which Americans routinely underestimate and which you can test out before buying, as at France) and the Hummel figurines (which appeal to some and not others). You can see them being made, which, as they're not cheap, may have to suffice. You might get almost as much fun watching the ones in the giant cuckoo clock, which emerge and run through their paces every hour on the hour. The glass and crystal here aren't any less expensive than anywhere else, but of astonishing heft, in some cases. The toys are very sturdy, although the name of the shop, Der TeddyBar, tells you something. Of course, if you really *want* your own cuckoo clock . . .

One of the "homeless" shopping vendors in the World Showcase is the West African–style **Village Traders** between Germany and China, which has sweet little carved animals and stylized figurines, beads, and a bit of leatherwork; but now that the Animal Kingdom has opened, it's a little outclassed. (Of course, if you don't have time to visit Animal Kingdom, then this is more attractive a stop.)

China is pretty seductive to shoppers: The classic architecture, taken from Beijing's Temple of Heaven, the amazing gardens, and 360° film tend to transport tourists into the perfect souvenir-hunting mood. The Yong Feng Shangdian store is willing and able to help. From the elaborately carved furniture, porcelain and inlay vases, and heavy fine rugs to the Susie Wong satin dresses, fans (some of them made on site), cotton slippers, chopsticks, tea cups, and lacquer boxes, this is one of the highlights of the lagoon's "left bank."

Norway's classic ski sweaters make it into the "Best Souvenirs" list; some of the jewelry is also striking. The mugs and trolls are *eeehhhnnn*—very cute, but very predictable. Does your aunt have a *tchotchke* shelf?

Mexico's serapes might have got in there with the outerwear of Canada and Norway, but for the fact that such items (we're speaking from experience) seem to lose their cuteness after a while, even among retro-hippie teenagers. Some of the silver jewelry is quite elegant and heavy, but again, the prices are not particularly lower than at another store (and nothing like what you can get on the street in a big city). If you're shopping for smaller kids, the stuffed burros, sombreros, and maracas are old reliables.

DISNEY-MGM STUDIOS

This park was made for memorabilia, of course: movie posters, "jeweled" sunglasses, autographs, and so on. Far and away the hottest joint in town is **Sid Cahuenga's One-of-a-Kind,** which is a combination of Starabilia and Reel Finds: antique movie premier tickets, many to Disney movies (the $5 ticket to *Fantasia* very nearly made it to the best souvenirs list), and star costumes. Some of this stuff is outlandish, of course, but who knows when the investment might pay off? No doubt Sonny Bono's $500 pink outfit doubled in value after his untimely demise. And if your significant other has a lifelong crush on Clark Gable or Jimmy Stewart, you have a fairly good chance of finding an autographed picture here. If not, check out **Legends of Hollywood** and settle for a video copy of *Gone With the Wind.*

If Cahuenga's price tags slow you down, there's the economy version, **Celebrity 5 & 10,** where vintage lunch boxes are more likely than custom lounging pajamas. **Buy the Book** is half-coffee shop, half-bookstore, and some of the bookstore part is lifted straight from the former set of the sitcom *Ellen*. And **Once Upon a Time** has Disney characters in some of the more intriguing forms, like under snow globes and on puppet strings.

The "hotel boutique" at the **Twilight Zone Tower of Terror** is a classic; aside from the robes (see "The Best Souvenirs in 'the World'," below), it has several haunted house–style gimmicks, such as rubber eyeballs and screaming boxes. It's hard to resist the Muppet menagerie at the gift shop near *Jim Henson's Muppet-Vision 4D* show. And for any *Star Wars* fan, the figurines and gear at **Star Tours** is prime stocking stuffer territory.

And for the guy who so truly has everything that he can afford to joke about it, look into the **Sunset Club** and see if the pocket watch with ears is still there.

ANIMAL KINGDOM

This is the newest of the theme parks, and with decades of marketing experience to go on, the Disney company has come up with some surprisingly smart souvenirs to stock it with, and for nearly every age group. Frankly, the one group of Disney creations that *aren't* for sale somewhere—the fantastic and whimsical animal-shaped benches, wall sconces, and lanterns that adorn the paths and buildings of the park—are among the most attractive objects in Disney World and would provide the basis for a really successful accessory catalog. Oh, well.

Island Mercantile, in the central area around the Tree of Life, has lengths of batik-printed cloth to wrap as you please, and some are already sewn into dresses; New Age music, some recorded over and under animal calls; and beaded earrings. Beastly Bazaar is jumping with *"It's Tough to Be a Bug!"* and *A Bug's Life* stuff, including the spunky little green guy who is rapidly becoming the Jiminy Cricket of the '90s.

Over in Africa, the connected **Mombasa Marketplace/Ziwani Traders** shops have a lot of good-looking carved wooden birds and animals, from small to several feet tall, along with reptiles with a surprisingly soft plastic "skin" that puts rubber to shame, plus walking sticks, zebra-striped and leopard-spotted candles, animals masks to hang on the walls, and "rain sticks" filled with rattling seeds. Among the best-looking clothing in Disney World are the cargo vests, very Banana Republic chic these days and sure to please the teens—and fairly inexpensive for their class at $38. The same safari fashions adorn Animal Kingdom Barbie, though the miniature version goes for $25. (Make sure you check out No. 11 on the "Best Souvenirs" list below before you leave the Harambe Village area.)

At Conservation Station's **Out of This World** shop, you'll find a lot of shampoos, shower gels, and soaps with nice smells and no-animal-testing guarantees, none of which is so unusual any more, but whose sales in this case partially benefit conservation organizations. There's snack food that fund them, too, so you can feel a little less guilty about downing the caramel-coated trail mix. Also look for adorable stuffed parrots and wooden animal puzzles with giant-sized pieces for toddler-sized playrooms and educational nature videos and books.

Chester and Hester's Dinosaur Treasures in DinoLand U.S.A. (see "Best Souvenirs," below) has T-shirts, sweatshirts, animal noses, and a lot of those dinosaurs with the soft but long-wearing and non-bruising skins that make even spines and teeth safe as child's play.

The Best Souvenirs in "the World"

Partly to show how clever Disney Imagineers (and concessions-sellers) can be, here is a baker's dozen of our favorite souvenir items available from Walt Disney World. As we pointed out before, price is no object to pleasure, but a good bargain never hurt anybody. (The $4 Mickey-face drawer pulls didn't make the list, although they came very close; that's a good example.)

Please remember that prices as well as merchandise selections change constantly, so some of these particular items may be out of stock or even out of production by the time you visit. But at least you'll have an idea of the possibilities. These are not in order of preference, so don't think you're "settling" for one instead of another.

(1) The "Hollywood Tower Hotel" terry-cloth robes from the hotel lobby "boutique" at the Twilight Zone Tower of Terror attraction in the Disney-MGM Studios. These are both well made—as good as those at any luxury hotel, where you'd pay more than the $58 these go for—and quite funny in a subtle way. If you had never been to Walt Disney World, you'd probably think these were a bona fide Beverly Hills item. If you have a guest bathroom to supply, this could be really funny. And if you honeymooned here, well . . .

(2) Buddy Holly's autographed guitar, one of several celebrity instruments for sale at the Starabilia store on Disney's West Side. Of course, its price tag is a hefty $18,500, so it's quite likely the most expensive souvenir in the World, too; but if you're a fan, you're a fan. A close second would be the B. B. King guitar, which, though not Lucille herself, of course, is nicely autographed for $4,995.

(3) The khaki-colored baseball caps, embroidered with a small but fine *T. rex* skeleton on the front and with an unusually subtle (especially for Disney) Disney's Animal Kingdom logo on the back. These are comfortable, attractive (they fit better than those dome-topped vinyl things), and only about $16; check them out at Chester and Hester's in DinoLand. The cargo vests mentioned above are a very close second.

(4) The leather Mickey armchair, the greatest media-room concept ever seen. Michael Eisner probably has several—and if he doesn't, he should. Black leather, sausage-armed, and with a rounded back cushion (no ears; that would be too obvious), it sits on taxicab-yellow round-toed "shoes." This is serious furniture, at least in the price department: $3,400 for the adult version and $1,450 for the mini- (and just lightly more Minnie-) sized kid's chair at the Art of Disney store in the Marketplace. But (and you can thank us later) there is also a blow-up plastic model, virtually identical, at Disney At Home for only $50.

(5) Mandarin-collar satin dresses and pajamas in Yong Feng Shangdian in the China Pavilion at Epcot. These are very chic again (for some of us, they've always been fun), and these are of better quality than the mall-chain versions.

(6) The irresistible Mickey teapot, a simple and guaranteed smile-provoking black bowl with a double-eared top and a saucer that has four fat little glove fingers. They're a steal at $18, available at the Gourmet Pantry and Disney At Home, both in the Disney Village Marketplace.

(7) The pearl rings at the Mitsukoshi store in the Japan pavilion. This takes a little explaining, because it's half–state fair midway game, half-souvenir. There's a lady there who lays out several dozen live oysters on a bed of ice. You pay about $14 for the chance to point out the oyster of your choice, and if there's a pearl inside when she opens it, you get to keep it. Your chances of finding a pearl are fairly good, as most come from cultivation farms, though only a few are of any substantial size. And then, of course, you have to have it set, which is where the shop makes at least some money, since the settings are already made (sterling, gold, or plated) and you pick one out. Still, it's fun; you can resist buying a ring unless it really is a good pearl (or buy one already made) and still have a fun souvenir.

(8) We proclaim a tie for cool-weather gear between the wool and fleece outerwear at the Traders of the Canada pavilion at Epcot's World Showcase and the classic sweaters at the Norway pavilion. Canada has the slight edge because of a greater variety of jackets, pullovers, and sweaters; and neither are particularly inexpensive, but both stock well-made and sturdy versions.

(9) Pottery—bright, pretty, and remarkably inexpensive—at the Moroccan pavilion in Epcot, along with sturdy, box-like woven baskets that are $12.95 here and that would cost you ten times as much in the Charleston market.

(10) The Mickey-but-modern desk accessories for the young-at-heart executive or home-office entrepreneur at 2R's Reading and Riting in the Disney Marketplace. These are unusually sleek Mickey shapes, including some nice two-lobed calculators and desk clocks; and for someone who's trying to write the great American novel, there's a little accessory box, good for paper clips, push pins, or whatnots, topped with a wooden Mickey hard at work at the (manual) typewriter and with his wastebasket full of crumpled drafts ($22).

(11) The soapstone animals carved by Kisii craftsman Jonathan Kioko in the open-air market of Harambe Village in the Animal

Kingdom. Kioko's carvings range from tiny to several feet, and correspondingly vary in price; you can get a lovely little hippo for $35, or spend a $2,000 for a large water buffalo or mother and baby elephant that would dominate a mantelpiece. And even better, you can usually watch the artist himself, sitting in some shade not far from the Tamu restaurant.

(12) For real Disney lovers, particularly those who have romantic attachments to the place, or even better, are getting married or honeymooning there, there's a way to proclaim your love to the world. No, you can't carve your initials in a heart into the Swiss Family Robinson Treehouse. (In fact, you couldn't if you tried; it isn't wood.) But you can have your names cut into one of the hexagonal bricks that lead up to the gates of the Magic Kingdom. For about $100, you can place those three little lines at her feet (among several thousand others, perhaps, but it's the thought that counts). You'll get a map, too, so you won't have any trouble finding it on your tenth anniversary. For information, call (800) 362-7425 or ask at the Guest Services desk.

(13) That black Claudette Colbert Chanel bag at Reel Finds.

Index